THE COMMANDMENTS

The Commandments

Ten Ways to a Happy Life and a Healthy Soul

SUSAN MUTO
AND ADRIAN VAN KAAM

CHARIS

Servant Publications
Ann Arbor, Michigan

Charis Books is an imprint of Servant Publications especially designed to serve Roman Catholics.

Scripture selections are taken from the *New American Bible*. Wichita, Kans.: Catholic Bible Publishers, 1992-93 edition.

Excerpts reprinted from *The Book of Concord*, edited by T.G. Tappert, © 1959 by Fortress Press. Used by permission of Augsburg Fortress.

Imprimatur: Most Reverend Donald William Wuerl
            Bishop of Pittsburgh
            May 13, 1996
Nihil Obstat: Joseph J. Kleppner, S.T.L., Ph.D.
            Censor Liborum

The Nihil Obstat and the Imprimatur are declarations that this work is considered to be free from doctrinal or moral error. It is not implied that those who have granted the same agree with the contents, opinions, or statements expressed.

Except where otherwise indicated, all stories appearing in this book are composites based on the authors' own experience and that of others, rather than true stories. Any reference to a person or persons living or dead is unintended and entirely coincidental.

Published by Servant Publications
P.O. Box 8617
Ann Arbor, Michigan 48107

Cover design: Hile Illustration and Design, Ann Arbor, Michigan

96 97 98 99 00 10 9 8 7 6 5 4 3 2 1

Printed in the United States of America
ISBN 0-89283-953-8

LIBRARY OF CONGRESS CATALOGING-IN-PUBLICATION DATA

Muto, Susan Annette
    The commandments : ten ways to a happy life and a healthy soul / Susan Muto and Adrian van Kaam.
      p.   cm.
    Companion volume to the author's Divine guidance, c1994.
    Includes bibliographical references.
    ISBN 0-89283-953-8
    1. Ten commandments.   2. Christian life.   I. van Kaam, Adrian L.   II. Muto, Susan Annette. Divine guidance.   III. Title.
BV4655.M87   1996
222'.1606—dc20   96-2925
                                            CIP

Contents

Introduction

MANY ARE THE TIMES when people put to spiritual guides the earnest question: "Can we know the true peace and joy in this life?" The answer is *yes* on one condition: "Do we believe that God intends for us a life of happiness?" Again the answer is *yes*. Our conviction of beatitude rests on the formula for a happy ("full of virtue") life and a healthy ("freed of vice") soul, a formula given to us by God. It consists of Ten Commandments, which we call the spinal column of the spiritual life. These are not arbitrary suggestions but divine demands.

Far from robbing us of our health and happiness, they guarantee it. We intend to show that the Decalogue offers still today the best set of pointers to peace and joy anyone could hope to receive. It was as if God knew that the people he had chosen to cross the desert into the Promised Land could not make it unless he gave them ten clear-to-follow directions, explicit commands that were both firm and freeing. He would even inscribe these Ten Commandments on stone tablets. Then he would ask one of the finest spiritual leaders the world has ever known, Moses by name, to teach them.

These divinely decreed commands are not for weaklings. Tough love, true love, tender love begins with God. There is nothing trivial about his commandments. They are humanly and spiritually formative because they are first and foremost the laws of God, not merely polite suggestions or arguable guidelines. Some readers may chafe at this kind of strictness, but an order is an order, especially when God gives it.

ABOUT THE AUTHORS

In this book we want to show to a wavering world the immense reservoir of spiritual and moral power to be found in the Ten Commandments. Fostering such a foundational approach has been the work of a lifetime. It began with the pioneering efforts of Fr. Adrian van Kaam and his friend, Rinus Scholtes, in Holland in 1936. They established in the Hague an informal association of Christians profoundly concerned with their spiritual character and personality formation, which also served as an ecumenical outreach to people seeking solid guidance in their life of prayer and social presence. This small faith group was to be the prototype of our present-day Epiphany Association.

Fr. Adrian was compelled to hide by the Nazi invasion of the Netherlands in 1944. While in hiding he helped many others, who had also fled to the countryside in order to escape deportation. With the missionary openness and compassion that has marked his entire faith and formation journey, Fr. Adrian devised ways to reach out to others who were suffering and in need of spiritual care, regardless of their church affiliation (or lack thereof). Appealing to the message of the Ten Commandments, which are written in the hearts of all people, he was able to touch the lives of the spiritually and physically abandoned, and to lay the groundwork for the pretheological formation science and the theology of formation which would be his life's work.

After the war, as a priest in Holland and a member of the Spiritan congregation, he was assigned to serve in the Dutch Life Schools for Young Adults, established in and around mills and factories. There he helped women and men, ages eighteen to twenty-four, who were seeking to piece together lives shattered by conflict, confusion, and chaos. He and his colleagues devised a unique approach to renewal by combining catechetical education with spiritual formation. Their aim was to teach people in everyday life how to integrate their faith tradition (what they believed) with their formation tradition (how to fulfill this belief and to find peace and joy).

When Father came to the United States in 1954, first to teach psychology as a human science at Duquesne University in Pittsburgh and then to found in 1963 the Institute of Man (later renamed the Institute of Formative Spirituality), he drew upon years of study, writing, and teaching in the recognized fields he had originated in the Netherlands: the science of formation and the comprehensive theology of Christian character and personality formation it serves.

Joining Father as a director and professor in this Institute in 1966, following an established editorial career, Dr. Susan Muto brought to this work in due course a special area of expertise. She combined the formative reading of classical spiritual literature with the findings of formation theology. For over twenty years, this partnership of gifts and talents served the graduate level training of over eight hundred laity, clergy, and religious the world over, who now hold leadership roles in their churches, in seminary and college education, and in a wide variety of ministerial positions in many denominations.

As colleagues and administrators in the Institute, we authored and coauthored seminal texts in these fields, taught and cotaught original courses, and guided master's theses and doctoral dissertations. In 1979, while the Institute was still flourishing, we launched what has proven to be the crowning point of our life's work: The Epiphany Association, a nonprofit research, publication, education, and consultation center headquartered in Pittsburgh. Since 1988, and especially since the closing of the Institute phase of our work in 1993, it has become our full-time commitment. Through our Epiphany Certification Program (ECP) and our ongoing formation sessions, with the help of a dedicated staff and excellent adjunct instructors, we serve Christian professionals, postgraduates, and all people dedicated to spiritual deepening and Christ-centered caregiving.

This book on the character-forming power of the Ten Commandments is a companion volume to the previous book we published on the Beatitudes, *Divine Guidance: Seeking to Find and Follow the Will of God* (Servant, 1994). Both books offer firm yet reachable goals for the renewal of faith, hope, and love through living an inspired, God-guided life.

THE TEN COMMANDMENTS: PROHIBITION AND PROMISE

We see the Ten Commandments as entry points to a lifelong course in the formation of character. Taken together, they are like floodlights in our dark nights of self-inflicted confusion where individuals and society as a whole seem to have lost sight of the clear choice between right and wrong.

The Ten Commandments are not ancient, undecipherable hieroglyphs. They are divine prohibitions that promise those who obey them admittance to a good, God-fearing way of life that brings with it much peace and joy. In this book we hope to bring to light their formative meaning, to show the link between these ancient laws and our everyday experiences in family life, in the workplace, and in our faith community.

Prohibition ("Thou shalt not") is merely the underside of the promise ("Thou shalt") of receiving God's peace in our own hearts and the joy of serving others. These are ten steps we humans have to take to forestall the destructive consequences of disobedience. Through obedience, we gain the freedom to become who God intends us to be.

Even people who do not yet know Christ know full well that they want less violence on our streets, more fidelity to family values, and a fairer distribution of our planet's goods for its inhabitants. All this can happen—if we follow the Ten Commandments step-by-step. Each one flows into the other and returns to the former. None ought to be obeyed in isolation. All are required if we want to grow both morally and spiritually. Teaching them takes time, living them involves hard choices that are ethically sound, but every day we obey, we make progress toward the blessed life.

Think of character formation both as moss gathering around a stone and as a moveable feast. Following the commandments requires stillness and motion, reassessment and progress. We take a few steps forward and at times fall behind, only to start again. No sooner is one commandment followed than the next one beckons. We endure slow days of regrouping and moss-gathering as well as feast days of spiritual progress.

Good character, virtuous and true, like a well-built home, cannot be crafted overnight, for the virtues of our character match the dispositions of our heart. They go to the deepest core of our Judeo-Christian personality formation. At the level of the heart, we can only mature spiritually in loving obedience to God and in accordance with the commandments he gave us. They are the most revelational and formational tools to be found anywhere on earth.

With Moses as his mediator, God presented the Ten Commandments—the Decalogue—to the Chosen People in the form of ten clear directives, unambiguous in their intent. We want to view them also as ten steps to basic peace and joy, tough to climb, demanding patience and time, but in every way worth the effort. These commandments, as recorded in the Old Testament (see Exodus 20:2-17; Deuteronomy 5:6-21), are completed in the New Testament through the witness of Christ and his teaching, especially in the Beatitudes (see Matthew 5:3-12).

Given the state of our world, where "my way" seems to prevail over any adherence to authority, it might seem strange to devote a whole book to human and Christian character building through the Ten Commandments. There are three reasons why we have decided to do so.

First of all, the commandments, to repeat, are like the spinal column of the spiritual life. The recent publication of *The Catechism of the Catholic Church* makes this truth self-evident. This comprehensive compendium of all Catholic doctrine regarding both faith and morals is built on four pillars: what we believe, what we celebrate, how we live, and how we pray.[1] The third pillar of *The Catechism*, pertaining to our life in Christ, devotes its entire second section, as we might expect, to the Ten Commandments.[2] Not surprisingly, we found that this ancient set of laws advances to the cutting edge of our own formative theological reflection on life's unfolding in a time of transition like our own. Relearning and reliving these ten steps is of vital concern to all people if we are to survive as reasonable, loving, trustworthy children of God and citizens of the earth into the third millennium.

Secondly, everyone, from religious believers to secular humanists, agrees that there is a crisis of values in our culture. Families are more broken than whole. Many young people live on the edge of despair. There seems to be a lack of meaning in life.

What has happened to the backbone of America? Why are there so many random killings? Why is armed robbery and petty thievery so common? Why are political networks so filled with lies, scandal, and corruption? In an atmosphere where people are morally separated from both the demands and blessings of the Ten Commandments, these directives make perfect sense. That is why recommitting ourselves to them can have a decisive impact on our devastated world.

The third reason we want to revisit the commandments as timeless keys to basic peace and joy is that we do not have to search far to find the treasures they unlock. God showed us the way with great clarity. Thus this book begins with the first of the Ten Commandments, which marks the initial step we must follow, and it ends with the tenth.

Complementing each chapter are selected readings from the literature of spirituality plus a set of reflection exercises designed to enhance the formation of our virtuous character. Each chapter ends, as does this introduction, with an original prayer-poem by Fr. Adrian van Kaam.

As you will see, one step along the way to a God-guided life leads to the next. All of them together give us a head start on the straight and narrow road to true happiness (see Matthew 7:13-14). From the beginning, God has had our salvation as his goal. All he asks is that we take these directives, written on stone, and carve them on our hearts.

There is no way we can express our thanks to the people who made this book possible, but we must commend in a special way our Epiphany Association staff and most notably our expert typist and administrative secretary, Mary Lou

Perez, along with her daughter, Sara, for whose tireless assistance we are deeply grateful. We are thankful as well to Servant Publications for the editorial help given to us, especially by Heidi Hess, and for the personal encouragement we received from Bert Ghezzi to bring this project to fruition with all its forming, reforming, and transforming potential.

We Adore You

We adore you
Perpetual spring of wisdom's words
That in sparkling accord
Echo against the mountainside
Thundering wild and wise;
Out of fire, cloud, and darkness dense
Your commands entered history's negligence,
Infected by idolatry.

We adore you
Mighty majesty descending
From eternity into passing time
To pour the heady wine
Of life divine
Into arid hearts and minds.

The burning blueprint,
Chiseled by your blazing hand
On stony tablets,
Binds us by golden cables,
Strong and long,
To the mighty wisdom
Of your mystery.

Thank you
For bright beacons commanding
Perilous passages through polluted seas
Threatening to drown humanity
In their raging waters.

Thank you
For the tree
On which Jesus bled in agony
To atone for the forgetfulness
Of the Father's message on Mount Sinai.

O Jesus, make us cling
To words in which we hear you sing
Of promised peace and joy
In nights of desperation.
Keep us faithful to your gifts,
Save our limping lives,
Let us not drift away
From the secure bay
Of your commanding love.

—Fr. Adrian van Kaam

O N E

THE FIRST COMMANDMENT:

*"I Am the Lord Your God:
You Shall Not Have
Strange Gods before Me."*

The Way of Adoration

He sends forth his command to the earth; swiftly
runs his word!   **Psalms 147:15**

Why would this "I am" description of the divine nature be the first step on the way to our character formation? The answer ought to be obvious. In telling us who he is, God reminds us in the first commandment—much to our humiliation—that we are not God. We may play God; we may craft our own golden calf; we may live in the illusion that we are in charge of our life, but we can never escape the truth of our ultimate nothingness. We are creatures. God is our creator. Our life is the length of a breath, and we have no ultimate control over it.

We are then told not to place any other "gods"—no stockpiles of power, no collection of possessions, no lesser pleasures—above the God who made us. This commandment is like the first vertebra of our spinal column. If it breaks, death or paralysis may result.

The spiritual consequences of breaking the first commandment are just as severe, and yet a great deal of idol worship goes on in our world. People place their sports and political games, their peers, their careers, even their cars before God. Idolizing is a common practice. Even believers fall victim. *My* friends, *my* fame, *my* finances may secretly enthrall me more than the God I ought to serve.

Disobedience to this commandment can take many forms, as subtle as they are deceptive. If this basic premise of faith crumbles or grows weak, our whole being may sink with it, and slowly die.

Unfortunately, even on this first step, when we hear the word "commandment" we feel defensive. People accustomed to having their own way do not like to take orders, not even from the Most High. A word less threatening to them, but powerful in its own right, may be "invitation."

The first commandment is a direct appeal to us from the Adored. God, our Father and Creator, loves us and invites us to love him more than any other person, event, or thing.

As we draw nearer to God, in praise and adoration, in awe and wonder, we rightly feel overwhelmed by his unspeakable magnificence. In the glow of love's radiance, we recognize our own human frailty. His strength becomes our security. We know we can stop play-acting and cast our allegiance with the only God worthy of the name.

Such surrender de-stresses our lives. It makes us feel better. It prompts us to do what is right and good. As long as we are on the way to obedience, we can be imperfect human beings and still find the happiness and harmony we seek.

To take this first step does not mean that we are anywhere near the end of the long road to the formation of a virtuous character. It means only that we are moving in the right direction. To build the distinctively human or transcendent personality God intends for us, we must use our freedom to choose the path he decrees. We must then try to stay on course, even if we fail many times to reach our goal. As long as we are heading in the direction commanded by

God, we can be sure of his help. The results will show up in the quality of our social, vital, and functional lives.

AN INVITATION TO CHANGE OF HEART

The Ten Commandments invite us, without forcing us, to mirror in our whole makeup the likeness of God in whose image we are made (see Genesis 1:27). Each step along the way enables us to live in fidelity to our call and in obedience to the Great Commandment to love God with our whole body, mind, and soul—and to love our neighbor as we love ourselves. Because we are free, we may choose the right way, but it is also possible for us to go astray.

People in AA (Alcoholics Anonymous) recall the day they hit bottom. Their world fell apart. They could no longer deny that their drinking had become their "god." Thanks to AA, they are able to aim with all their heart on becoming free from this addiction. The harm it has caused to themselves and others has to come to an end.

It takes a great deal of courage to take the first step—to name one's idols and then to smash them for God's sake. Even though an admitted alcoholic decides to stop drinking, he or she may experience a relapse. But all is not lost. To overthrow an idol the first time is to turn a corner. To seek one's true God is to make a good start.

People in recovery know they must renew their intention not to give in to their craving every day. When their promise holds, the One praised for this grace is God. The first step to freedom requires admitting one's problem; the second step requires a total reliance on God. This is the same as saying: Obey the first commandment and do not put "strange gods" before God.

Once we take this step, we feel already renewed. The fire of love for God alone begins to burn in our hearts. Our character starts to change for the better. We may take a few detours, but the disposition to be on course guides us to the right road. Slowly on, as the intention to let God be God takes first place in our life, good things follow. We soon feel happier, more peaceful, joyous, and full of life.

Character formation "through Christ" is an admission that we cannot succeed by ourselves alone in this work of divine craftsmanship. The Messiah embodies the mystery of saving love. Jesus' firm yet gentle presence is the avenue to our transformation. To follow him means not only to live the commandments, but to be disposed to become fully Christlike in our character.

Under the guidance of the Holy Spirit, our Comforter and Advocate, whom Jesus gave us as his parting gift, we begin to reform our inner lives. Our way of thinking, feeling, remembering, and imagining becomes more God-guided than self-centered. This inner reformation spills over into an ongoing transformation of our deeds and dispositions. Thus the forming and reforming power of the commandments has a transforming effect on our world.

The prohibition in this first step (to place no "strange gods" before God) leads to the continual reminder of our dependence on God's never-ending supply of grace. By cultivating adoration as a lasting disposition of the heart, we are more likely to stay focused on the Adored. This awe-filled disposition affects all the virtues of our character. We become more Christ-formed, more obedient to God's commands out of love, not fear.

The appeal of this and the other nine commandments operates at the level of the heart. We are directed to listen affectionately, not to reason argumentatively. Paying attention to God's commands arouses awe and affective longings. We want to bow down before his sovereign majesty. We want to be more humble and truthful about who we are.

When the Chosen People in their stubbornness refused to obey Yahweh, their hearts became hard. The golden calf they built symbolized their stony interior; it matched their disaffection from God. That is why Moses smashed it. Only then did the children of Israel repent. Only then did they try to develop dispositions of discipleship.

INVITATION TO ADORATION AND INTIMACY

The text of the first commandment is both simple and shadowed by mystery: "I am the Lord your God." There is no other "god" with such attributes of immanence and transcendence. Though he reveals himself to us in creation, God's essence is and remains veiled. His presence permeates the whole universe. His cosmic epiphany shines in the stars and the planets, in sun, moon, earth, and sea. Tremendous as the universe is, God leaves his traces in the smallest atom, in every cell of our bodies. "Fear not, be not troubled: did I not announce and foretell it long ago? You are my witnesses! Is there a God or any Rock besides me?" (Is 44:8).

This first invitation to moral and spiritual acquiescence and integrity can only be accepted if we bow down before a divine mystery so deep we can never fathom it. We must stand in awe before the One whom we cannot see or touch, but in whom we believe.

Christianity adds to this strong directive the message of mercy. We are sinners. We often miss the mark. God forgives us. He understands when we fail to go in the right direction. He asks only that we cultivate the disposition of adoration and make the decision to get back on track.

The formative meaning of this commandment becomes clearer when we focus on the word "your" in the initial invitation, "I am the Lord *your* God." It is a word of tender intimacy. It captures the awesome truth, disclosed in Holy Scripture, that God has loved us first. God calls us by name. We are his chosen.

The I-you bond between us and God points to the humility inherent in this divine initiative. God did not have to give himself to us in this way, yet he revealed with force and intimacy the truth of his fidelity and love. We are called to oneness with God from the beginning to the end of time. It is as if God were saying to us personally:

When you were a baby, I already knew you. From the first to the last I had a special destiny in mind for you. I formed you with an unrepeatable character. You are here on this earth because nobody else can possibly be for me what you can be. "I am the Lord YOUR God." I know you and call you by name. I have counted every hair on your head.

To worship or adore anyone or anything more than God is to shun intimacy with God; it is to violate the divine initiative. To love God with our whole soul, mind, heart, and will is to accept his invitation to adoration. To respond to his call is to answer to his appeal for intimacy.

God reaches out to touch us. He loves us first, so much that he literally carved his heart's care for us on tablets of stone. He burst through the cosmos on Mount Sinai and gave his freeing laws to Moses for our benefit. He did not have to do so. God could have kept these secrets of happiness to himself, but he chose to share them with us. Are we ready to listen?

DO WE LOVE THE LORD "WITH ALL OUR HEARTS"?

It is said in Scripture that we are to love the Lord our God, "with all our heart and with all our mind" (Mt 22:37). This means that where God is, there must we be—not in part, nor halfheartedly, but with all our strength, energy, and attention.

Consider for a moment the word "all." It is a small word, yet it has immense implications. There is nothing wimpy about how God expects us to respond. "All" does not mean once in a while, nor does it imply that God can have a little piece of us—but not more. God is not satisfied if we dole out our love like dewdrops. He demands another response—not arbitrarily, but because he is worthy of being loved with the whole of who we are. Only then can our character be formed in accordance with the first commandment.

OBSTACLES TO ADORATION

There are two primary obstacles to our wholehearted adoration of God. The first is a divided heart; the second is a prideful heart. As we consider each hindrance in turn, ask yourself whether or not you need to come to terms with them in your own life.

A heart divided. What if ours is a divided heart? What if we love God only halfheartedly instead of wholeheartedly? The first commandment compels us to ask:

> *Where is my heart? In my work? With my friends? Does it belong to God—or to a world that thinks it can survive without him? Do I give God a little piece of my heart here, a small portion of it there, but never the whole? Is it possible for this broken, wounded heart of mine to be made complete if I give God my all in all?*

God will not settle for anything less than the whole of us. This call to oneness with the Most High is the founding stone laid by the first commandment for the entire edifice that will become our virtuous character. It is like the cornerstone of an architectural masterpiece. Imagine God's disappointment when we choose instead to erect a shoddy edifice or craft an alien thing to idolize.

> *How can my people do this to me? I want to make of them a chosen race. I desire to bestow on them every imaginable gift and grace, and what is their response? Each and every time, they choose other gods. They do not give me their whole heart; they do not give me their whole soul; they do not give me their whole mind. How could I love this people any more than I do? I give them laws to set them free and they choose bondage. I give them everything they need and still they resist and refuse my love, building false gods I have to destroy.*

If we give the Adored all that we are and do, if we allow him to release us from the bondage of self-love, we may find more peace and joy than we could have ever imagined. The whole of us, our core form and its expression in our character, will then be set free. We soar on wings of grace to new, life-giving levels of intimacy.

To love with the whole of us means to give God our hands and our feet, our senses and our spirit, our gifts and our talents, with no holds barred. Such love is rightly seen by poets and prophets as wild and passionate, but to those who are lukewarm or willing to settle for leftovers, such love may appear to be fierce or even frightening.

Adoring God on this level of loving abandonment transforms our character. It makes us more open, gentle, gracious, and strong. We are better able to resist vice and choose virtue. We take the "narrow way" known to saints and mystics. We long for intimate communion with God. Our character seems less dispersed and more integrated, for where "I" leaves off, God begins. Such oneness is a true gift. It represents a firm *yes* to the universal call to holiness.

Nothing needs to be hidden from God. He already knows us through and through; he loves us despite our sinfulness, for he tells us, "I am... your God." It is as if God says to us:

I want you to love me until there is no separation between us. Trust me. Nothing is going to be taken away from you. Rather everything you seek will be given to you, but on a level much deeper than you can possibly grasp. Only learn to adore me above all others. Stand on the solid ground of humility, not on the shifting sands of false pride and deceptive self-sufficiency.

A prideful heart. In the Book of Chronicles, we find an excellent example of virtuous character building in King Asa (see 2 Chronicles 14:1-14). During the ten years of his leadership, Israel was at peace. He decided from the beginning of his reign that he would do exactly what the Lord asked of his people in the first commandment. He would not allow any false god to be raised in place of God. He and his subjects would live in adoration and obedience.

At the end of ten years, coinciding with the end of Asa's reign, all was well—that is, until he made one fatal mistake. He did not realize that the real test of his character would entail not the smashing of heathen idols, important as this was, but the smashing of the idols in his own heart. As the Book of Chronicles relates, Asa did not rely on God to help him win the battle. He began relying on Asa. The minute he did so, the break he had dreaded occurred between him and God. For King Asa raised up the largest idol of all: his own pride.

Notice well. At the start Asa did what was good and pleasing to God. He removed the heathen altars and the idols on high places. He broke to pieces and cut down the sacred poles that paid homage to gods and goddesses other than the God of Abraham, Isaac, and Jacob, the God whom the people had been commanded alone to adore. Asa commanded Israel to observe to the letter the law God had decreed.

There is a lesson for us in Asa's story. As we try to craft our character in the shape of the person God wants us to be, it is good to check out whether or not we have the courage from the start to see into our prideful heart and remove this idol of idols. What are the pagan altars we have unwittingly built up within our lives? Are they altars to material goods? To having everything go our way? To tempting God to conform to our bargains and demands?

Whatever the idol may be, are we willing to break it into bits, as Asa initially did? Consider your answer carefully. When you smash an idol you have built, it will hurt your pride. When you cast aside your self-woven security blankets, you may feel painfully vulnerable. When your life shatters into pieces, you may be whiplashed by anger, self-pity, and a sense of defeat. But learn to trust the process of divine transformation. God can make something beautiful out of even broken bits if we agree to wait upon the mystery. Soon we may see in these obstacles a formation opportunity.

CONDITIONS FOR ADORATION

Just as there are two conditions that prevent us from adoring God as we ought, there are two primary antidotes to this "sin-sickness."

Moving from false pride to true praise. We will never advance to deeper levels of spiritual health unless we are willing to disclose those areas within our heart where we still worship false gods or (like Asa) refuse to trust enough in our God. The rough edges of distrust and self-absorption need to be smoothed. Are we investing too much of what belongs to God in that which is less than God? This may be the most difficult question we have to face. Answering it requires great candor.

What areas of everydayness are not yet under the guidance, rule, and domain of God? What aspects of our private, relational, or devotional lives need to be brought under his lawfulness and loving care, lest they alienate us from true adoration?

As we have seen, the main force opposing this posture of humble presence is false pride, not a superficial kind of boasting or showing off, but a much deeper problem. Pride is the basic inclination to believe that "I" or "we" can do it alone. People with this problem often harbor beneath the surface of such brash behavior a lot of hidden fears and feelings of insecurity. They need to control things, so much so that pride, understood as total self-sufficiency, gets the best of them.

Such pride is at the root of our fallen human condition. It is the original sin described in Genesis. It was not enough for Adam and Eve to be like God; they would be "gods." The result of their disobedience in eating the forbidden fruit was not joy but despair, not peace but disruption. The myth that "I" on my own power can make "myself" whole is a sure formula for failure. Placing false gods before God banishes the possibility of intimacy with the Divine, and therewith, of true happiness.

To move from false pride to true praise means to love God as our first priority and to admire, never abuse, the good people and things God has made—the friends and family around us, the challenges that face us, the gifts the Adored grants us. We must first praise God if we are to survive as a people, humanly speaking. This praise is only possible if we do not hold on to lesser goods too tightly. To be willing to let go is not easy. We must try to swallow our pride and praise God if we want to enjoy the happiness of an undivided, humble heart.

A first condition for living this commandment is that we stop trying to play God. There is no shortcut to obeying God's will in our everyday life, no shout from heaven, only a continual, prayerful reading of the signals God sends to light our way on this first step to peace and joy.

Remembering that we are forgiven. Sometimes it takes a good fall to keep us humble, to remind us of how much we rely on God. Where God's love is, there forgiveness abounds. We are weak. We fail. At the same time, we are of good will. The remembrance that God is merciful keeps us at peace. It fills us with joy. We are not afraid to admit that we are human after all.

We can go to the Adored, all the while knowing that we have been forgiven. Before the world began, God had in mind a plan to save us from our fallenness by sending his own Son to save us. Through the power of this first commandment, we come to realize the fact of forgiveness. It becomes more possible to be at ease and in touch with God, even when we sometimes fail to live in obedience. We still know, because God tells us so, that he loves us with an everlasting love, and that he gives himself to us through Jesus.

The first commandment is like a beacon shining in our lives. It helps us to define our limits and to face the reality of loss and love, of the cross and the resurrection. Along the way, we meet the best and the worst we can be. Self-knowledge is not always pleasant, but it is necessary to overcome the myth of self-sufficiency. To say with the saints, "My Lord and my God," is to live in obedience to God's call and his command. It is to let God imprint these words on our character with his mighty hand:

I am… the only God you will ever need. I alone can lead you to wholeness. I seek from the start a personal relationship with you. You don't need inferior representations of my majesty when you can have me. Let your character be transformed accordingly. Take this beautiful world I have given you and be good stewards. Work in it. Play in it. Enjoy wisely its beauty and abundance. Only keep my name holy. Remember in your involvement to set aside a day to recall from where the world came. Then our friendship will be assured. You shall be my people, and I shall be your God.

TIME TO REFLECT ON
THE FIRST COMMANDMENT

Step One: Adoration

God, as the poet Francis Thompson suggests, is like a "Hound of Heaven." He is pursuing us at every moment. He longs for us to seek him with all our heart, with all our soul, with all our strength, and with all our mind (see Luke 10:27).

We must have no other gods besides God. When we are rightly and uprightly aligned with the Holy One, when he has first place in our lives, other constraints fall away, other distractions take their place—a distant second.

Dethroning our idols—whatever they may be—through obedience to God's will and purpose draws us to a place of rest. Disobedience produces stress and strife. The way to a happy life and a healthy soul is paved with the "golden bricks" of adoration, intimacy, praise, and obedience.

The first commandment thus forms our hearts in awe-filled love for God alone. In the words of Martin Luther, from *The Book of Concord:*

> The purpose of this commandment... is to acquire true faith and confidence of the heart, and these fly straight to the one true God and cling to him alone.... To have God, you see, does not mean to lay hands upon him, or put him into a purse, or shut him up in a chest. We lay hold of him when our heart embraces him and clings to him. To cling to him with all our heart is nothing else than to entrust ourselves to him completely. He wishes to turn us away from everything else, and to draw us to himself, because he is the one, eternal Good.... Let everyone,

then, take care to magnify and exalt this commandment above all things and not make light of it. Search and examine your own heart thoroughly and you will find whether or not it clings to God alone. Do you have the kind of heart that expects from him nothing but good, especially in distress and want, and renounces and forsakes all that is not God? Then you have the one true God. On the contrary, does your heart cling to something else from which it hopes to receive more good and help than from God, and does it flee not to him but from him when things go wrong? Then you have an idol, another God.[1]

QUESTIONS FOR REFLECTION

1. What prevents me from offering to God my wholehearted love? Am I honest about my known faults? Am I willing to change them? Are there areas of my life where I have given in to pressures and temptations that have gradually overtaken me? Do I use my tongue to criticize or judge others, to gossip or exaggerate? In what way do my words bring or not bring praise to God and his creation?

Your Thoughts:

2. Can I name the "idols" I have erected so far in my life? Do I allow the media or other people to distract me from loving God above all things? Do I misuse my body by indulging in the "gods" of alcohol, drugs, or sexual misconduct, or by overeating, failing to exercise, or working myself to death? Do I have the courage to remove these false gods from my life, to smash these idols into pieces, as Moses did?[2]

Your Thoughts:

3. What areas of my life are not yet under the guidance, rule, and domain of Jesus and his Holy Spirit?[3]

Your Thoughts:

Worship of You Alone

Thank you for beseeching me
To bend my knee
To bow before your blazing throne
To give my heart to you alone.

My spirit, mind, and loving will
Light up like candles white and still
Venerating Father's will.

Unwind my restless mind,
Remind my aching heart
That from the start
You were merciful and kind
To me, your wayward child,
Who did abide in foolish pride.

You lifted me with tender hand
From exile in a land
That did not understand
Why I should worship you alone,
Not Egypt's gods of wood and stone.

Faith, hope, and love
Spring up in me
To temper my idolatry.
If faith grows weak
In the grinding round
Of pain and care,
You keep me still aware
Of your gift of strength

To prevent, to mend,
Cavities of doubt and heresy,
That eat away the certainty
Of any lonely heart.

In days of darkness
When hope grows dim,
You refresh my tired soul,
You show me how to cope
With my despair.

Recall then your care,
Your pledge of leniency.
You wipe away so tenderly
My stream of tears.
You soothe my sorrow
Opening up a new tomorrow,
With snow as white
And bright as laser light.

Above all, my Adored,
Bind me with the shining cord
Of love that takes away
The sting of sin, the cruel play
Of frigidness, tepidity.
Transforming me into a worshiper
Of only thee, O Holy Trinity.

—Fr. Adrian van Kaam

T W O

THE SECOND COMMANDMENT:

*"You Shall Not Take
the Name of the Lord
Your God in Vain."*

The Way of Veneration

If you obey the commandments of the Lord, your God, which I enjoin on you today, loving him, and walking in his ways, and keeping his commandments, statutes and decrees, you will live and grow numerous, and the Lord, your God, will bless you in the land you are entering to occupy.

Deuteronomy 30:16

From the first commandment, adoration of God as the most sublime presence in our lives, the second commandment naturally flows: to venerate his holy name. This invitation, along with the first (not to place false gods in the way of the deepest intimacy and love God wants from us for himself alone) and the third (to keep holy the Sabbath) disclose a foundational set of life directives, different in intention, yet somehow alike. They call us to craft our characters in the likeness of the One in whose image we have been made.[1]

God initiates a deeper relationship with us through adoration ("I love you"); through veneration ("I bless your name"); and through dedication ("I honor you on your day and every day").

With the second commandment, God peels away one more layer of the mystery veiling his luminous being by

39

referring to his name. A fuller knowledge of God is not attainable on our own. That is why we need revelation or divine information to guide our character formation. The commandments are nonnegotiable agreements made between God and us. They propel us beyond a limited adherence to divine rules and regulations. Understood as loving guides yet firm directives for the unfolding of human existence, they force us to think about the course of our life.

On this second step of the ladder to true happiness through obedience, the Lord tells us that we are not to take his name in vain. This is like saying,

My love for you is so great that I deserve your respect. I have called you into being, and I will be with you always. So I tell you, don't take me for granted by taking my name in vain.

VENERATE THE NAME OF THE LORD

The second commandment invites us not only to proclaim the holiness of the Lord's name but also to venerate God as our Creator. A basic facet of character unfolding has to do with our giving God the reverence he deserves because of who he is. In personal conversation, in family life, in the workplace, and in churches, where the name of God is uttered with reverence, there is an atmosphere of veneration and prayer.

To keep the name of God holy is an expression of praise and appreciation for his creative majesty, his merciful love, his sanctifying presence. The more we revere God's name, the more likely we are to penetrate the mystery to which it points without ever exhausting its meaning. For, in the words of St. Augustine, cited in *The Catechism:* "[God's] name is great when spoken with respect for the greatness of his majesty. God's name is holy when said with veneration and fear of offending him" [2149].

NAMING: AN INVITATION TO DEEPER INTIMACY

To honor someone's name suggests that we know that person intimately. In many ways, our name is who we are. So, too, is God's name who God is. God tells us his name because he wants us to know who he is. It is "I am who I am," in Hebrew, "Yahweh." To know God's name, to dare to utter it reverently, is to find ourselves at the threshold of new levels of intimacy. By veiling his unspeakable splendor, while still revealing his name, God made a rightful claim to our reverence while entering into a here and now relation of at-homeness with us. The Almighty could have remained aloof, above it all. But the second commandment assures us of his desire to break through every barrier to intimacy. God entrusted his name to the Chosen People, which means he gave them some knowledge of himself. He expected and deserved their respect.

Consider the power of the Jesus Prayer in Orthodox spirituality: "Lord, Jesus Christ, Son of God, have mercy on me, a sinner." The prayer names Jesus as Lord, as the second person of the Blessed Trinity. It also names us as sinners in need of redemption. We feel closer to God when we say it. From within this Trinitarian circle of love, we can face our weakness and ask for forgiveness.

Properly venerated, the name of God can stir deep feelings in us. It can touch and transform our heart. We give God many names because no one name can describe who he is. He is the Mighty One, our Rock, Emmanuel, Prince of Peace, Advocate, Comforter. All three Persons of the Trinity are named throughout the course of salvation history. Every name carries its own appeal to know and love God more.

The same goes for our name. It is a source of knowledge. It discloses something of our character as reverential or as sinful, as committed to veneration or as prone to vulgarity.

Be quiet for a moment. Pause from the hectic pace of life. Place yourself consciously in the presence of the immortal One. Hear his holy name in your heart. Let it match your breath. Draw life from it. Then, reconsider the second commandment. Hear in it that God wants to befriend you. Be still and know him as your God (see Psalms 46:11) because he has told you his name.

VAIN NAMING AS AN OBSTACLE TO INTIMACY

What is our response to this appeal? Sinners as we are, we often take God's name in vain. We seem oblivious to the sacredness of its expression by mere mortals like us. We forfeit our second chance to attain lasting peace and joy by not disciplining our way of speaking about so wondrous a God. The language of love can never be constricted by vain and thoughtless naming. It is expansive, freeing, and profoundly festive. The rhetoric of vulgarity, as opposed to veneration, makes us immune to scurrilous expressions, rough and abusive words.

Respectful naming creates a climate of peace. People feel more trustful of one another. A family that watches its language enjoys more peace than one where hurtful words are more the rule than the exception. We no longer believe in the children's rhyme: "Sticks and stones will hurt my bones but names will never hurt me." They do.

The vain use of God's name has many repercussions in our personal life and in our world. Lack of respect for the name of God is a sign that our heart has hardened and that as a people we are fast slipping away from a sense of the sacred. The dispositions of reverence and respect are in danger of disappearing. The name of God is used irreverently on street corners, in the movies, in popular music, almost everywhere people gather. All of us have to pay the price for this vulgarity. It kills our sensitivity to God's presence. When respect for the name of God declines in a culture, the entire culture declines with it. It's as if we are drowning in violence and vulgarity. Yet hope springs eternal because our God is so good.

For example, even people who use God's name in a thoughtless way change their tune in an emergency. A physician we know told us that the word most often on people's tongues when they come into the emergency room of his hospital is "God." "Oh God, why am I here? Oh God, why did this happen? God, please don't let me [my husband, wife, child, friend] die."

A litany of desperation transpires in the waiting room. When people have to face all at once pain, fear, guilt, and final questions about life, the only word they may be able to say is "God." Whether it is an expression of deep faith or only a spontaneous utterance is not always clear. But it's often the only way people who haven't prayed for a long time come to prayer. The name of God in these situations is not necessarily taken in vain. It means something. If nothing else, it acknowledges that there are times that are so desperate, one may not survive them without help from on high.

On good days and bad, God beseeches us not to treat him caustically or casually. Whatever the occasion may be, he says gently yet firmly to us:

Don't pretend I'm not important in your life. Don't you know by now that you need me for every breath you take? Don't use my name insultingly. Keep it holy.

FRUITS OF VENERATING GOD'S NAME IN EVERYDAY LIFE

If our name is important to us, imagine how much more important God's name is to him. We find, when we read the writings of saints and spiritual masters, that the nearer they grew to God, the more intimate were the names they whispered to him. With each name they experienced another facet of God's mystery. They wanted to name it, yet no expression could adequately capture what they had experienced.

To Francis of Assisi, he is "My Lord and my God."

To John of the Cross, he is "My Beloved."

To Catherine of Siena, he is the "Sea of Peace."

To Teresa of Avila, God is simply "My Friend."

The essence of God transcends any name we can find; yet he wants to communicate the mystery of his presence to us. We can only be with him in a person-to-Person encounter when we have a name for him. Before he can teach us this name, he has to command us to venerate it.

The name of God has to bear fruit in our everyday life and world. It has to be in tune with each stage of our spiritual unfolding. In childhood we might name God our Protector; in adolescence we may think of him as our Counselor; in adulthood as our Heart's Longing. Our sense of maturing spiritually parallels the ripening fruit of veneration; God keeps forming, reforming, and transforming our life and world from moment to moment. He is the Lord of heaven and earth. When we imprint his name on our hearts, we acknowledge his nearness to us and we grow accordingly.

God's infinite, mysterious presence, once named by us, is at the same time awesome and accessible. His love attracts our heart and gives us new life. We express a multitude of feelings in the one word "Lord." It begins to reverberate throughout our character. Our personality radiates the goodness of his name.

When we say "Lord" in the course of our daily prayers, we find that it taps a wellspring of loving affections and affirmations of joyful dependency, venerations for an all-powerful mystery that bows to our misery. Every time we move, speak a word, or take a breath, we know with newfound certitude that it is only because the Lord holds us in being. It is God who gives strength to our hands, direction to our hearts, endurance to our will. Holy is his name!

We say "Lord" both when we stand still in awe and when we dive into our work. We say "Jesus" when we take care of our children, clean house, plan meals, work at the computer, drive the car. We realize we could not do anything, from the toughest task to the most insignificant chore, were it not for the sustaining presence of God. His mighty power, his all-pervading mystery, sustains our mundane world.

The prophet Jeremiah, mouthing the words of the Lord, says, "Call to me, and I will answer you; I will tell to you things great beyond reach of your knowledge" (Jer 33:3).

We respond to these glad tidings not with lengthy explanations but by saying with faith, hope, and love, "The Lord is his name."

As the disposition of veneration becomes continuous and lasting in our hearts, its fruits abound. The Lord begins to tell us great and mysterious things about himself:

> The days are coming... when I will fulfill the promise I made to the house of Israel and Judah. In those days, in that time, I will raise up for David a just shoot; he shall do what is right and just in the land. In those days Judah shall be safe and Jerusalem shall dwell secure; this is what they shall call her: "The Lord our justice."
>
> **Jeremiah 33:14-16**

So all-pervading is God's love for us that he outpours the power of his name in his only-begotten Son, our Lord Jesus Christ. His is the name that will help us to reform our deformed lives. He will save us from our sins. "The Lord our justice" is truly a name to venerate!

The psalmist echoes this ecstasy: "O my strength! your praise will I sing; for you, O God, are my stronghold, my gracious God!" (Ps 59:18). God is the rock in whom we trust. Even in the darkest night, he is there for us. At these times, let this be our prayer:

> *Lord, I am living under great stress. It feels as if there is so much I need to do. Hear me in my distress as I call upon your name. There are problems wherever I turn, yet I feel the power of your sustaining presence. Thus, I call upon you to be my strength, my fortress, my refuge, and my rock. Steady me in these discouraging moments. Walk with me to places of new hope. Your name is to me justice, mercy, and love.*

FINDING THE "RIGHT NAME" FOR GOD

Our experience often matches the names we choose for God. These names are not theological definitions but descriptions rich in mysterious powers of transformation. They enable us to enter into the experiential depth of this second step to peace and joy. To find the right name for God in the right situation is to deepen the sense of loving togetherness we want to enjoy with the Most High.

It is like the bond between two married people who love each other dearly. Over a lifetime they find terms of endearment, special names for one another, only they know. They use these names to express in shorthand a tender moment of marital affection. Naming one another in this way makes them feel embraced and truly at home.

God gives us a name (Adam, Eve, Isaac, Jacob, Esther, Ruth, Mary, Joseph, Peter), and we give him a name (Father, Prince of Peace, Advocate), and in that naming we find each other. Naming ought to uplift, never diminish. Names are not empty terms; they are pregnant with meaning.

We learned a good lesson in this regard from a friend who was with her nephew shortly before his eighth-grade confirmation. The other children had gone to sleep, but he was restless. She asked, "What's bothering you this evening?" He said, "I don't know what to do! I have to pick my confirmation name and I don't know what it should be. Why don't you pick a name for me?"

Sensing that this was a teachable moment, our friend replied, "There's no way I can select your confirmation name for you because the Holy Spirit has to be your guide. The name you choose for yourself is your decision. It might even have something to do with the spiritual direction of your life. When you came into this world, your parents chose your baptismal name. The Sacrament of Confirmation offers you a chance to decide what name you want. What saint would you like to have as a role model?"

Her nephew looked puzzled. Then he said, "If it's that serious, it's no wonder I can't make up my mind!"

"Do you remember the book I bought you on the lives of the saints?" asked his aunt. "Go through it and read about a few lives that appeal to you. Then wait. I know the Holy Spirit will help you find the right name for yourself."

Before she left he asked one more question. "What was your confirmation name?" She told him it was Veronica. "You mean the woman who wiped the face of Jesus on the way to Calvary?"

"Yes, that woman inspired me when I was a young girl. She had courage. She was not afraid to do the right thing. It took guts to push through the crowd, risk the anger of the soldiers, and wipe the face of Jesus, who was suffering so much."

"Who else was there?"

"Well, Simon of Cyrene helped him carry the cross."

"Maybe I should take Simon."

"Go to sleep! Naming is important—but not at midnight!"

As it turned out, the boy chose the name "Michael," asking the archangel to protect him from wrongdoing and open his heart to the gifts of the Holy Spirit.

A PATTERN FOR CHARACTER FORMATION

The second commandment follows a common pattern seen in all ten steps toward character formation. It moves between prohibition and promise, between "don't do this" and "if you do as I say, good things are going to happen to you as a result."

This commandment prohibits using the name of God in an abusive way. It forbids false oaths, blasphemy, swearing, and similar aberrations. It promises to put into place not only in our heart but also in our corresponding character the basic virtue of veneration. With veneration comes an increase in our sense of the sacred, plus a decrease of disrespect and the violence, cruelty, and sheer lack of courtesy that accompany it. Together with these virtues, we receive a heightened sense of our creatureliness.

Saints and spiritual masters believe that the first and foremost disposition for growth in holiness is humility. To say God's name reverently is to profess that we depend on him for everything. We place nothing, certainly no false idols or vain names, between us and the Holy. Humility cancels disrespect for God. It seals the bond between our veneration and God's blessing. In a way, all the commandments include the first two, for adoration of God and veneration of his name are the motivating forces behind our mature choices. Why else would we keep the Sabbath or honor our parents or refuse to lie, steal, cheat, kill, or covet?

When we lose veneration, the effect on character formation is always detrimental. In demeaning God, we demean our chances to grow in holiness. We become insensitive to the sight, the sound, the touch, the feel, the very scent of the sacred. When vain naming takes the place of veneration, this lack of reverence extends to other areas of life as well. People begin to take lightly their promises and commitments. The phrase "I give you my word" may be empty of meaning if we do not venerate God's word.

Mystics like St. John of the Cross tell us that we have to go through a "dark night of the senses"[2] if our receptors to veneration are to be purified of the dust and debris of irreverent attachments to that which is is less than God. We cling so tightly to things named as ours (*my* looks, *my* career, *my* things) that we fail to place first the name of God. Blinded by our own vanity, we miss the epiphanic manifestations of the holy in the midst of our everyday life. These are God's names, his signatures, as it were. But when we lack veneration, we fail to recognize their abiding beauty.

Respectful presence to the name changes this bleak picture. Veneration as a character-forming disposition enhances our ability to catch the traces or names of God everywhere in creation.

St. John of the Cross in heightened moments of ecstatic absorption said that his Beloved is like "silent music" and "sounding solitude," like a "supper that refreshes, and deepens love."[3] All these ways of naming God are only similitudes. They echo his attributes while hiding his infinite Being.

The name of God has about it an inexhaustible depth. By contrast, when Scripture speaks of the devil, the evil one, it says that his name is legion. Satan changes his name to accommodate whatever deception is afoot. The name of the Lord, our God, the name we are not to take in vain, is simple, yet in it resides a bottomless abyss of love and beauty. It is the name above all names, the name at which every knee should bend (see Philippians 2:10). We can almost see the devil dancing when he hears the Lord's name taken casually. Vulgarity knows no bounds.

MOVING FROM VAIN NAMING TO RENEWED VENERATION

What can we do to change this corrosive climate? That's where character maturation comes into play. To follow this second step, we need to check our own language before we condemn the language we hear. Are our own speech patterns in tune with veneration of the sacred, especially in casual circles? Reformation of bad habits, such as the constant use of pejorative language, will make us more sensitive to the wider implications of this commandment. We must not let certain kinds of music, films, and humor desensitize us to the sacredness of God's name.

Connected with any name are meanings that are either transformative (sublime, sacred, venerable) or deformative (vulgar, sacrilegious, hurtful). The latter breed depreciation and negativity. Take a name like that of Adolf Hitler. Even to say it is to conjure up images of indescribable cruelty, concentration camps, and persecution. Or take the name of a legendary figure like Dracula, a name that connotes dark thoughts and ancient fears.

These examples illustrate that some names incline us to see the good, others connote its opposite. To block bad naming, we might try meditating on the prayer that Jesus taught us. As soon as we say, "Our Father who art in heaven" (adoration), we immediately add, "hallowed be thy name" (veneration). This is like saying, "May your name, O God, be sanctified, respected, and celebrated."

When we pray the name while walking in nature, something else may happen. We comprehend with contemplative certitude that no name can contain the wonder, greatness, and beauty of our heavenly God. Everything—budding flowers, singing birds, frolicking squirrels, sparkling stars—all connote names for the Creator we venerate. All communicate something of the abundance of his love.

The maturing of our virtuous character can go on all day long if we hallow, celebrate, sanctify, and glorify the name of God. We can keep his holy name in our heart and mind by simply remembering the prayer of St. Francis of Assisi, "My Lord and my God." Everything we do can be done for the sake of his name. All that we are, all that has life and being through us, is due to his name, for without his name neither we nor these things would be. There would be no flowers, no birds, no squirrels, no trees, no people. We would not be able to move, speak, work, plan, or dream of the future.

Everywhere we turn, we can see and meet something that names the Trinity. The flowers name God's beauty, the birds his freedom, the animals his strength, the trees his immensity. Ice and snow name him. Rain and sunshine name him. All sing of our Creator God. Everything in nature, all life forms and most of all we humans, flow from and are sustained by the mystery we name God. In this way veneration becomes a character trait. Our prayer life becomes more full and deep. Our spiritual formation unfolds into a life of divine transformation.

In the New Testament, Jesus reveals his knowledge of the second commandment and explains it further. In the context of the Sermon on the Mount, in Matthew's Gospel, Jesus teaches us a new lesson about this second step to inner serenity:

Again you have heard what was said to your ancestors, "Do not take a false oath, but make good to the Lord all that you vow." But I say to you, do not swear at all; not by heaven, for it is God's throne; nor by the earth, for it is his footstool; nor by Jerusalem for it is the city of the great King. Do not swear by your head, for you cannot make a single hair white or black. Let your "Yes" mean "Yes" and your "No" mean "No." Anything more is from the evil one.   **Matthew 5:33-37**

Swearing here does not refer to what happens in a court of law when one swears to tell the whole truth and nothing but the truth. Here the Lord explains how terrible it is to use God's name in vain. It diminishes the power, the beauty, the strength, the greatness of his epiphany within world and humanity.

If we swear by other things, by heaven, by earth, by Jerusalem, we begin to say that we have the authority to elevate these places or things to a godlike status. We almost idolize them, and that would violate the first commandment. Therefore, Jesus says in no uncertain terms, "Don't do such a thing."

In Jesus' time, as well as in the present age, people in high places may lie, steal, cheat, and mock the mystery. This lowering of veneration for the Most High trivializes human dignity. It breaks our communion with God. It would seem in this light that the second commandment is a call to reform our language. If language is the "house" in which character unfolds, then anything deformed in it needs to be both reformed and transformed.

Consider a small child. He or she begins to speak the language learned from father and mother. Then, slowly at first, one imbibes the jargon of the neighborhood and the school, then the rhetoric of one's country of origin, and so on. Each language, be it of family, neighborhood, school, or country, is different. From the time when words first pass our lips to when we breathe our final breath, language forms our life. A German feels different from a Spaniard or an Italian because of the language he or she learns. An American feels different from an Englishman or a Kenyan because of the idiom in which he or she was raised.

In other words, just as we have a house to live in, decorated to suit our taste, so we also have a language that becomes our house of formation or, for that matter, of deformation. Language houses our thoughts, feelings, memories, and imaginations. It is the site of willing and deciding on a good or bad course of action. Our field of formation as a German, a Spaniard, an American, a Dutchman, or an African is what it is because of the language that shaped us while we were growing up.

That is why we must be careful with the language we use. Does it foster or demean our distinctively human spirit? Just as our childhood home continues to influence us, so language imprints itself in our mind and heart in vain or venerable ways.

We must never underestimate the forming, reforming, and transforming power of the word. It affects us without our even knowing it. This is especially true in regard to the language of the sacred. Any language that belittles the sacred lowers all meaning. This is a heavy price to pay for breaking the second commandment, but it will be exacted whenever desecration replaces veneration.

When we diminish the sacred, life as a whole loses its

savor. People in pain have nowhere to turn, no faith-filled name to call upon. They ask, "What is the meaning of it all?" When God's name sustains us, we learn from experience that there is more to life than meets the eye. We take another step toward lasting peace and joy. We behold in the name of God love and wisdom, power and might, mercy and compassion—enough to embrace all the hurts in the world and open the door to lasting happiness.

That is why we must choose with care the language we use and pass on to others. It is what keeps us mentally alive and spiritually inspired. Because language is the house of formation, the dwelling place of the whole and holy, we ought never to use any sacred word, especially the name of the Lord, idly or frivolously. To do so is to diminish the integrity of the language God himself has given to us. It lasts when other words are lost.

TIME TO REFLECT ON
THE SECOND COMMANDMENT

Step Two: Veneration

God's name is holy. How we treat its disclosure is a sure indicator of where we are in our development of character. Do we heed this call and respond to it respectfully, or do we belittle or ignore it?

Reverence for the name of God reflects a heart set on him and his ways. Irreverent or vulgar behavior indicates a flaw in our character formation. Veneration is a refining step we have to take to ensure further spiritual unfolding.

Among all the words of revelation, there is one which is so holy it is almost unspeakable: the name of God, "Yahweh"— I am who I am. To believers God confides his name. He reveals his personal mystery through the prophets (see Jeremiah 33:1-16), as well as the greatest mystery of all: that we are each called by name. As we read in Isaiah (43:1): "I have redeemed you; I have called you each by name: you are mine."

The second commandment insists that we reverence the name of the Lord in faith-filled abiding. In the words of Martin Luther from The *Book of Concord*:

Unfortunately it is now a common calamity all over the world that there are few who do not use the name of God for lies and all kinds of wickedness, just as there are few who trust in God with their whole heart.... God at the same time gives us to understand that we are to use his name properly, for it has been revealed and given to us precisely for our use and benefit. Since we are forbidden here to use the holy name in support of falsehood or wickedness, it follows, conversely, that we are commanded to use it in the service of truth and all that is good.... Thus his name is hallowed, as we pray in the Lord's Prayer,... for true honor to God's name consists of looking to it for all consolation and therefore calling upon it.... Many a terrible and shocking calamity would befall us if God did not preserve us through our calling upon his name. I have tried it myself and learned by experience that often sudden, great calamity was averted and vanished in the very moment I called upon God.[4]

QUESTIONS FOR REFLECTION

1. Do I call upon the name of the Lord when I am in trouble or do I try to take charge of things myself? Have I ever used the divine name to my own advantage, for example, by taking an oath under false pretenses? By swearing, blaspheming, or joking about sacred words and symbols to call attention to my own importance and cleverness? By profaning God's name instead of governing my way of speaking? By committing perjury? By taking an oath with no intention of keeping it?

Your Thoughts:

2. What names do I reserve for the Lord alone? Is he for me the "Righteous One" or the "Prince of Peace" or simply, "My Beloved"? What makes me take God's name in vain? Anger, irritation, fear, impatience? The need to prove that I'm a down-to-earth, no-nonsense person? How can I overcome this bad habit? How can I place my name under the jurisdiction of the name of the Lord?

Your Thoughts:

3. What can I do to assure that God's name is used by myself and others for honorable purposes only? How can I offer God the respect owed to his revealed name and the sacred reality it evokes? How can I teach others—children and adults—to venerate the name in silent, loving abiding as well as in words of blessing, gratitude, praise, and glory?

Your Thoughts:

Mighty Name, Immortal One

Rain mercy on this arid race,
We play yet pray before your face
To peel away what veils the mystery
Of your lovely name, O Trinity.
Let us proclaim
The wonder of that saving name,
A star that never shines in vain.

Make our heart flower
Into a sparkling tower,
A fountainhead of praise
Each time we see its trace
In flower, tree, or loving company,
In sky and field and mighty sea.

May we not turn away
From the festive tray
Of gifts and graces
Meeting us as mild oases
In the deserts of the daily grind,
Lighthouses that remind us:
The pain of our journey is not in vain,
If guided by his precious name.

Invitation to intimacy
With the name Divine
Imprinted generously
In space and time,
Mighty name, Immortal One,
Emmanuel, come, O come,

In our daily Israel.
You are the well in which we dwell,
With our everlasting name
Known to you alone,
Written on a white and shiny stone,
The hidden name we shall be told,
Crossing the bridge of biting cold
The final suffering of young and old.

Rising into the glowing spring
Of your embrace,
I am welcomed by the bell
Of my secret name
Sounding melodiously beyond the shell,
Muffling its ring in my earthly days,
Lost on weary ways
Of lust, of power, money, fame,
In idle search of the splendid,
Name of names finally
Disclosed to me,
The name concealed
In his divinity
Throughout eternity.

—Fr. Adrian van Kaam

T H R E E

THE THIRD COMMANDMENT:

*"Remember to Keep Holy
the Lord's Day."*

The Way of Dedication

*Thus says the Lord: Stand in the court of the house
of the Lord and speak to the people of all the cities
of Judah who come to worship in the house of the
Lord; whatever I command you, tell them, and
omit nothing.*   **Jeremiah 26:2**

Despite the emphasis in Western culture on materialism,
we observe among young and old a growing hunger
for something more meaningful. Christians of all faith group-
ings are trying to identify the source of this spiritual hunger,
to focus less on overcoming denominational differences and
more on reclaiming our common Judeo-Christian roots. The
third commandment, step three on our journey to peace and
joy, addresses our mutual commitment to keep holy the day
of the Lord.

THE SABBATH: A TIME TO REJUVENATE

Given the frenetic pace at which we live in Western society,
no one needs to remind us of our need for rest and restoration. It is ludicrous to think that we can "serve the Lord with
gladness; come before him with joyful song" (Ps 100:2)
while ignoring the Sabbath.

People push themselves, even over the weekend, to get more done. They find that they are even too overwrought to enjoy their vacation. Exhausted by abnormal stress and overwork, many agree it is time for a change. A remnant of faithful souls are expressing their longing for uplifting worship. There are signs of renewed dedication to liturgy, word, and sacrament in many churches. Small faith groups meet across the land for prayer, Bible study, and formative reading. People want to share their story of faith, their vision of hope, their call to love. They see the need for reformation, renewal, and revitalization. They are convinced it is possible to live every day as a day the Lord has made, to "be glad and rejoice in it" (Ps 118:24).

One parish leader put it this way when we spoke with her: "The Lord is preparing the way for a rebirth of dedication to his glory, his name, his day. Sunday brings sunshine into our life. The time is coming when it will shine all week long!"

In the word "day" there resides a wealth of human wisdom and experience. There are special days throughout our lives when we recognize our gratitude to God. Sometimes our thanksgiving is joy-filled, as on the day you were married or the day your child was born. Other times gratitude may be tinged with sorrow, as on the day God called a loved one to eternal life. On still other occasions, what we feel is simply an inner recognition, a burst of appreciation, for God's loving care for us. Remember the day you took off from work to enjoy a quiet respite, to make a retreat or simply to recreate with a friend.

All these days in our single and married lives are made by the Lord to bring us nearer to him. Sunday, his and our Sabbath, is set aside in a special way for prayer and play. This day is a pointer to our lifelong dedication to be a chosen race, a royal priesthood, a people set apart (see 1 Peter 2:9).

In the Judeo-Christian tradition, the Sabbath is meant to be a day of solemn rest where persons alone and in community remember the Lord. The Sabbath gives us pause to recall that we are human "beings," not human "doings."

When we dedicate ourselves before God to a time and space of pure presence, when we purposely halt our restless activity to foster the life of the spirit, we experience benefits throughout the week. In moments of contemplation we celebrate the deepest "for what" of our being.

From the beginning, ages before we were conceived in the wombs of our mothers, we were already alive in the mind of God (see Psalm 139). Classical Christian traditions teach that our essence in God precedes our existence in time. The dictum of formation theology is *Anima forma corporis*, meaning the soul forms or "besouls" the body—our whole thinking, willing, remembering self. We have a place in God's tender, compassionate heart. He loves us and calls us by name.

In other words, our essence has been preformed in God's heart and mind before we received our life or our existence as we know it here and now. The divine mystery of love, so to speak, loved us into being. It is God's love for us that we remember on the Sabbath. That is why we keep it holy. As the called and Chosen People of God, we are to first rest in him (contemplation); then we are to go out and bear fruit that will last (action). Such dedication is the only way to halt the desacralization of our time, symbolized so vividly by the violation of Sabbath rest.

RISING TO NEW LEVELS
OF TRANSCENDENT AWARENESS

How can we become aware that we are in God and God is in us if we don't set aside any time as sacred? We are destined to be on earth only for a little while. Whatever we do or accomplish, it will not be enough. God wants to give us a foretaste of the everlasting Sabbath we shall enter for all eternity. To deny ourselves this privilege is to disobey the third commandment.

The time we live on earth is meant to be a preparation for this perpetual day of the Lord. The third commandment helps us to see this day in the light of eternity and eternity in the light of this day. The Sabbath, properly lived, can lead us to a new level of transcendent awareness. It offers us a time when time slows down. It enables us to ponder and to celebrate the deepest meaning of creation.

From the moment of conception to our last breath, our preformation in God becomes a formation in time. We are created. Our essence comes into existence. Our birthday, viewed from the standpoint of formative spirituality, is also a day of consecration to the Lord. The Sabbath reminds us that we have been created by God and consecrated to God. We are to lead a holy life here on earth in anticipation of a life of unsurpassed holiness, peace, and joy in the life to come.

Keeping the Sabbath helps us to see God's plan for our personal and communal life. We must never allow sin to cloud our awareness of God's commitment to our salvation. The Creator of all so loved the world that he sent his only begotten Son to save us. It is as if the honor we give to God on the Sabbath is but a shadow of the honor God has shown to us. At least once a week, in some worshipful context, we ought to give the Lord the chance to say to us:

> *I know it is difficult for you to believe in a love as great as*
> *my own, but see, I am the Lord of mercy. For your sake I*
> *allowed myself to be nailed to a cross. Blood flowed from my*
> *hands and my feet. From the wound in my side, water and*
> *blood streamed out to signify my compassion for you, for I am*
> *your Redeeming Lord.*
>
> *My mercy knows no bounds. It is so great that I forgive*
> *and forget your trespasses. Turn to me. Sink into the abyss of*
> *my forgiveness. My people have sinned against me. They have*
> *hurt me by their lack of trust. Can't they see that I became a*
> *victim on the cross for their redemption? Listen to the com-*
> *mandments of my heavenly Father and trust in my mercy.*
> *Count on my forgiveness. Keep holy the Sabbath so that the*
> *messages I have for you may be heard by you.*

RENEWAL OF COVENANT LOVE
IS COUNTERCULTURAL

The Sabbath is also a day to celebrate with Israel our liberation from the bondage of Egypt, that is to say, from the
imprisoning power of sin. The Sabbath is a time to renew our
love-bond with God, the covenant he initiated between us.

Keeping the Sabbath holy is a way to remind ourselves
that we are not autonomous, self-sufficient beings. The truth
is, we belong first to God. This holy captivation becomes a
liberation from a consumer driven, materialistic world. In the
light of this third step to peace and joy, we must ask: What
does it look like to be Sabbath people?

In a society where time is money and achievement is the

highest goal, keeping the Sabbath holy is countercultural. As persons dedicated to God, we must learn to live in the world without buying into its merely secular values, morals, and ideals.

This does not mean that we have to be odd, or funny, or weird. It does mean that we must be conscious of "checkpoints." Going along with "the way things are" is fine, but only up to a point. Then we feel some other force drawing us away from the born-to-shop mentality and warning us to wait a minute.

We recognize a deeper call. We wager that there is more to life than all work and no play. We want to pray intently not only on the Lord's day but also while we participate in the workday world and take time for recreation.

Sometimes, especially when we are out and about in the world, keeping the Sabbath appears to be a waste of time. But when we get older our tune changes. Now the call to be countercultural seems to be happening at an even earlier age.

The nephew of a friend of ours came home one day after school, upset and aggravated. He blurted out to his parents, "Why did you make me be a Christian?"

"What's troubling you?" they asked.

"Why did you teach me things the other kids in seventh grade don't seem to care about?"

It turned out that there had been an incident of cheating in his classroom. He realized that he couldn't go along with what everyone was doing.

"Why did you do that to me?"

Whatever his parents said to him reconfirmed their Christian dedication and his, too. As Sabbath people we cannot do certain things we know in our hearts to be wrong.

THE SABBATH IS LIFE-GIVING

Another aspect of character formation in dedication reveals a lighter side of the Sabbath. It is not a time, as Jesus said, to kill joy but to give life. Jesus admonished the Pharisees that God did not make man for the Sabbath, but Sabbath for the man. He said in Luke's Gospel: "I ask you, is it lawful to do good on the Sabbath rather than to do evil, to save life rather than to destroy it?" (Lk 6:9).

Sometimes our misunderstanding the true purpose of the Sabbath causes us to resist it. Consider the story of this young boy, whom we'll call Billy. Billy's mother was a stickler for detail as far as religion was concerned. She insisted "under pain of sin" that he attend church every Sunday, no matter what. Billy had no choice but to go, and his resentment toward religion was building to the breaking point.

Billy's father noticed his son's attitude, and realized that he had to correct the boy's misunderstanding of what it meant to "remember the Sabbath." One spring day Billy's father saw his opportunity. He took his son to a Saturday evening service, and the next morning the two of them went fishing.

There was a calmness to the morning, a special quality to the Sabbath light neither one of them would ever forget. Billy remembered the way the trees, swaying in the wind, were reflected in the water. His father's words were etched on his heart: "God's world this wonderful morning is bright with life. It's good to be here with you, Son." This was liberation. This was where the two of them belonged.

Until then, Billy's image of God had been a wrathful tyrant looking over his shoulder—not a loving, inviting Father saying, "Come and celebrate this day with me. It is good for you to be with your father. When I was a boy like you, I went fishing too."

Years later, as a young man, Billy recalled with tears in his eyes that his father's decision taught him more about the Sabbath than he might have learned had he been forced again to go to church "at the time we always go."

For Billy and his father, the Sabbath that morning was an experience of the wideness of God's mercy. Together they saw something of the splendor of a deeper mystery in the open road, the farmyards, and the young corn coming up in clean, cultivated fields. This Sabbath moment wasn't confined to church; it was happening here and now.[1]

The Sabbath must continue beyond the time set aside for formal ritual. It is an experience of God's epiphanic presence in the world. That spring morning Billy discovered that the Sabbath had to do with God's goodness, with his father's sense of adventure, with the old fishing hole down by the mill. God's world was big enough to include people who both keep the Sabbath and know the joys of going fishing.

WORSHIPING GOD IN SPIRIT AND IN TRUTH

Of course, our freedom in Christ does not relieve us of our responsibility to be a part of the body of Christ, nor does it license us to forsake communal worship. However, keeping this day holy has to mean more than filling up the pews in church. Sitting in your customary pew like a plank in a sawmill to fulfill an "obligation" does not embrace the spirit of the Sabbath any more than a periodic fishing trip signifies its warning. This is not to suggest that the Sabbath is only a time for recreation. Attending church out of love for God is essential. But to take this step to happiness and harmony, we need to be present to God within hallowed walls as well as in open spaces. We need to keep alive on the Lord's day a spirit of adoration and veneration, of wonder and worship. Such dedication is undoubtedly countercultural, but so, too, is the third commandment.

There is a danger we need to mention in regard to the emerging interest in spirituality. On the one hand, grace seems to be leading people to a new sense of how necessary it is to find our happiness in God. There is a call to worship in spirit and in truth, and to not lose ourselves in substitutes for the transcendent, such as drinking and taking drugs or working ourselves to death to make more money. The "So what?" question is being asked by many these days. As one tycoon wrote in a popular airline magazine we read en route to a speaking engagement, "So what if I have two yachts? How many can I water ski behind?" A reformation of life, a rededication to God's way, is indicative of a genuine search for lasting peace and joy.

On the other hand, in a society like ours people grow up with the expectation that they ought to be able to master everything, including God's mystery. We are used to behaving in a forceful way. The language people choose gives us a clue to their need for excessive control: "*I* want to *have* a spiritual life." It sounds the same as saying, "*I* want to *have* a new car or a bigger house." Even the life of the spirit succumbs to the rhetoric of self-centeredness and possessiveness. Secretly, it's as if we would like the commandments to be products of our own doing rather than responses to God's initiative.

It is difficult for "controlling types" to change their style of listening to God's word, from asserting "rights" to becoming more receptive, and hence allowing our old, worn-out ways to be reformed. We may not see that the Lord is in the lead, and that his ways are not our ways. For example, Christ, who many called "Rabbi," castigated the Pharisees for so rigidly regulating the Sabbath that they forgot the balm of mercy. Their brand of dedication to law and order was deadening. It killed joy and eroded peace. In the name of religion they took the life, the liberty, and the beauty out of the Sabbath.

Religion is not meant to be a rejection of the body and its need for recreation, nor is it merely a collection of dry rules. At times God does speak to us in the heart of darkness, but even then, even in spite of the crosses we must endure, his Sabbath of light, life, and love awaits us.

In the lives of the saints, we see a veritable kaleidoscope of ways to honor the Lord's day. In the beginning, Christian, outbursts of piety were hardly tame. In pursuit of the transcendent, some sat on pillars for a lifetime, practicing a special "stylite" type of asceticism. Others, being more down-to-earth, followed desert fathers like St. Anthony of Egypt to pursue a life of virtue through moderation. His philosophy was to bend the bow but not break it.[2] Though a disciple might fail many times, Anthony knew with Jesus that the Sabbath was made for man, not man for the Sabbath (Mk 2:27-28).

The message the Lord wants to reveal to us through his saints and through this third commandment is that Sunday—or, for that matter, any day of the week—is always the Lord's day, provided we remember his presence and return to him. What counts in the long run is not this or that achievement but the crosses we carry for God's sake and the new level of dedication to which they bring us. No matter how many

Sabbaths we miss, we can make up for them if we are truly repentant. The secret is to ask God for the grace to grow more pleasing in his eyes. Then life on earth will ready us for an eternity of Sabbath experiences.

CELEBRATING THE SABBATH TOGETHER

St. John Chrysostom, an Eastern church father, shifts our attention from the personal meaning of the Sabbath to its importance in the faith community. He is quoted in *The Catechism* as saying:

> You cannot pray at home as at church, where there is a great multitude, where exclamations are cried out to God as from one great heart, and where there is something more: the union of minds, the accord of souls, the bond of charity, the prayers of the priests [2179].[3]

Alas, in many churches in the West, the functional mentality has taken precedence over the needs of the faithful. That may be why what we witnessed in Africa, while on speaking engagements there, was so amazing. Worshipers danced with abandonment, waved their arms, and sang with sheer joy. They brought fruits and flowers to the altar, embraced each other, and called aloud to the Lord.

Some African students we know say that going to church here is for them like entering a mausoleum. Even when parishioners are invited to exchange the greeting of peace, they do so without passion. The students see this ritual as an invitation to celebrate their loving fellowship in the Lord on his special day. We sympathized with their disappointment that people in church behaved so coldly.

There is a parish we love to visit in a predominantly African-American neighborhood. People come from all over the city to celebrate the liturgy there because it is so full of life. They attend worship out of conviction, seeking a Sabbath to remember. Visitors are greeted warmly. Before and after Mass, people talk to each other. They respond to the call to volunteer with enthusiastic dedication. They are revitalized, renewed, and made ready for the week in a truly Sabbath spirit that is beautiful to behold.

We need a faith community to help us to remember the Sabbath and keep it holy. We need to be together with people who feel as we do. Otherwise our churches risk emptying out. Mere organizational efficiency will not fill them. The Holy Spirit, animating our human spirit, instills in our character the dispositions we need to keep the Sabbath holy.

As children we used to play a game with our fingers. We said, folding our hands in the normal fashion while raising our index fingers, "Here is the church and here is the steeple, open the door, but where are the people?" Then reversing our fingers inward, because it was Sunday, we'd say, "Here is the church and here is the steeple. Open the door and there are the people. Close the door while they pray; open the door and *they all walk away.*"

The purpose of this third step to peace and joy is to overcome the split existence so pervasive in our world: to worship one day of the week but to "walk away" for the rest. Perhaps what the third commandment asks us to remember is that we are called to be people who are always, in some fashion, living the Sabbath.

The point of this *remembering* is not only to remind us to honor God on one official day but also to *re-member* ourselves to the Sabbath character of our faith formation so that we may become more holy.

As we move into the next millennium of Christianity, this remembering might take the form of witnessing to the day of the Lord wherever we are. We do not hesitate anymore to ask God to let his light shine through our personal and familial lives.

What if on Sunday, when everyone seems to be using the time to catch up with work, we dedicated ourselves to resting in the Lord, not just for the hour spent in Church, but for the entire day? How can we say we keep the Sabbath and still let Sunday be the day to get all our errands done? Is it possible for people to change in a consumer-oriented world? We don't believe so, unless they take to heart the third commandment, no matter how busy they are.

Some people, of course, have to work on Sunday—nurses, security personnel, sales clerks. Others have to work any day of the week they can to make enough money to live on. These necessities have priority, but such cases do not preclude the truth that people who focus only on "doing" or "having" may be missing the presence of mind to rethink their priorities.

To what are we dedicated? If there is no difference between the Sabbath and every other day of the week, then what tradition do we have to pass on to the next generation? Take a hard look at the faces of people in the pew, and the answer may be obvious.

When we become Sabbath people, we don't walk away from the church; we walk away with the church in us.

Character formation in Christ requires that we make the practice of personal and communal prayer a daily occurrence; that we stay on the alert for any occasion to show compassion for our neighbor; that we make faith, hope, and charity the hallmarks of our dedicated life.

In an interview shortly before his death in 1984, Fr. Walter Ciszek, S.J. said that as our prayer life grows and deepens, God is able to reveal himself to us more and more.[4] He is able to come to us in a new way. He gets past certain barriers we may have erected unwittingly and makes our heart his dwelling place. He shows us what we need to know to follow our life call to become Sabbath people in a busy world.

The first three commandments, like the Great Commandment, teach us to love the Lord our God with our whole soul, heart, body, and mind. We must not put false idols before God or take his name in vain. We must remember the Sabbath. The remaining seven commandments teach us what the second part of the Great Commandment asks of us: to love others as we love ourselves. We must be willing to share what we have and to care for the needs of others. This charitable dedication is the lasting, formative effect the experience of living the Sabbath ought to imprint on our character.

TIME TO REFLECT ON
THE THIRD COMMANDMENT

Step Three: Dedication

In a world where we never seem to have enough time to do everything, where we are told that it is better to be busy than to waste time doing nothing, this divine directive risks falling on deaf ears. Yet, because "being" exceeds doing, we are called to set apart a day of dedication to the One who made us. We receive a foretaste of the eternal Sabbath of the soul, the ultimate form of peace.

Society's plot against the Sabbath must be halted purposefully and irrevocably within ourselves. In keeping the Sabbath, we are restored both physically and spiritually. We heal the "split" in our lives between the religious and secular worlds.

The sacredness of this day for the Chosen People is likely, therefore, to arouse in all of us a good dose of spiritual guilt! We learn in the Book of Nehemiah (8:9-10) that the Sabbath is a day for resting (from work) and for rejoicing (in the gifts God has given us):

> "Today is holy to the Lord your God. Do not be sad, and do not weep" (for all the people were weeping as they heard the words of the law).... "Go, eat rich foods and drink sweet drinks, and allot portions to those who had nothing prepared; for today is holy to our Lord. Do not be saddened this day, for rejoicing in the Lord must be your strength!"

On this day we do not just go to church as a duty; we worship God as a joy. God gave us the Sabbath as a day for rest and rejoicing—not for depleting our energy but for repleting it. The third commandment reminds us that our socio-historical, vital, functional, and transcendent formation depends on our giving due honor to the day of the Lord.

In *The Book of Concord,* Martin Luther responds to the question, "What does it mean to keep holy the Sabbath?"

Nothing else than to devote it to holy words, holy works, holy life. In itself the day needs no sanctification, for it was created holy. But God wants it to be holy to you. So it becomes holy or unholy on your account, according as you spend the day in doing holy or unholy things.... Indeed, we Christians should make every day a holy day and give ourselves only to holy activities—that is, occupy ourselves daily with God's Word and carry it in our hearts and on our lips. However, as we have said, since all people do not have this much time and leisure, we must set apart several hours a week for the young, and at least a day for the whole community, when we can concentrate upon such matters and deal especially with the Ten Commandments, the Creed, and the Lord's Prayer. Thus we may regulate our whole life and being according to God's Word. Wherever this practice is in force, a holy day is truly kept. Where it is not, it cannot be called a Christian holy day.[5]

QUESTIONS FOR REFLECTION

1. In a culture where rampant consumerism is commonplace, how can I keep holy the Lord's day? When was the last time, discounting necessary work and travel, that I made Sunday a day of solemn rest—a day for being, not doing? For going for a walk instead of washing the car?

   Your Thoughts:

2. In a world where the sense of loneliness and alienation plague so many, where people often feel like lonely ships passing in the night, do I appreciate what it means to gather with an assembly of worshipers to celebrate the Sabbath both as a memorial of Israel's liberation from the bondage of Egypt and as a time to rejoice in our redemption by the saving love of Jesus? Do I thank God for his forgiving word in my life or do I take his presence for granted?

   Your Thoughts:

3. Do I believe with Jesus that the Sabbath is about celebrating life, not killing joy? It is about showing mercy as much as honoring God? Do I see the difference between fulfilling a Sunday obligation and living under the sign of an irrevocable covenant to praise God and his redeeming action in my life? How can I help others to see the Lord's day not as a casual or routine happening, but as a foretaste of the Sabbath banquet God has prepared for us from the beginning?

Your Thoughts:

Sabbath Song

Lord, on Sabbath day
Let my troubles fall away,
Leaving behind the pace
Of worn out weekly days.

Enjoy a day of restoration,
Of wonder, worship, adoration.
Throughout the Sabbath
Hear God's hymn:
"Enjoy me as a refreshing spring.
I love you so, come back to me
This Sabbath, let me set you free.
I am your home, your hiding place.
You are channels of my Sabbath grace.

"Let flow through you my charity
To those in pain and poverty.
Kindly care; warmly share
The burdens people bear
In hours tedious and long,
Thrown into the endless throng
Of busy beavers, bustling bees,
Swarming in cars, on bikes and buses
To the stern enclosing structures
Of office, school, and company,
Their life less restful, calm and free.

"Wherever leads your weekly way
Bring always with you Sabbath day.
Abide with people tired, bent,

Who have no dwelling place, no tent
To hide away, to heal
The pressures of the daily deal.

"Pray for those who have to labor
Serving hospital, public safety, transportation,
Even on their weekend day.
Pray in synagogue, church, and temple
That they, too, may find some semblance
Of stillness, peace, respite,
An inner Sabbath rite
To which I all invite."

— Fr. Adrian van Kaam

FOUR

THE FOURTH COMMANDMENT:

*"Honor Your Father and
Your Mother."*

The Way of Submission

My son, forget not my teaching,
keep in mind my commands;
For many days, and years of life,
and peace, will they bring you.

Proverbs 3:1-2

This commandment affects the formation of virtuous character at every stage of our life. When we were infants, it was essential that our parents honor us. If they had not believed in us, had great hopes for us, and loved us enough to provide for all our needs, we would have been lost.

With the onset of adolescence, with its peer pressures and striving for independence, the trusting bonds of childhood are put to the test. Cutting the ties between parents and children begins in puberty. In a loving atmosphere, children grow up wanting to honor and obey their parents, but they do not want to be either overdirected or overprotected.

In the best cases, the bridge to adulthood follows a normal, healthy course of nurturing and letting go. In the worst cases, where children have been physically abused, orphaned at an early age, or pushed too quickly to make adult decisions, they may run away from home either literally or symbolically—for example, by escaping into a fantasy world. Such youngsters are easy prey for those who promise to care for them, but who instead subject them to abuse or servitude that violates human dignity.

Whether we are single or married, pursuing careers or raising families, the invitation and demand of the fourth commandment persists. If our parents have tried to be loving, despite their human imperfections, they deserve to be honored as well as we can. We give our parents help and respect not only out of a sense of charity toward them, but also as a way for us to maintain our own integrity.

CHARACTER FORMATION
THROUGH SUBMISSION

"Honor your father and your mother." The disposition this commandment imprints on our character is that of submission. To honor the two people to whom we owe our lives, especially if they have honored us to the best of their ability, is to acknowledge our dependence on them and on God. Honoring is more than a matter of obligation or duty; it demands humility.

The beautiful witness given to us by biblical families—Abraham, Sarah, and Isaac; Joseph, Mary, and Jesus—signifies the centrality of this commandment. In these Old and New Testament examples, the Bible affirms that respect demonstrated between parent and child fosters the path of an individual's graced destiny.

Besides the willingness to submit to legitimate authority, people in family and community have to be open to and forgiving of one another. They need to let go of the hurts of the past, practice compassion, and find a way to make a new start even in difficult relationships.

For clarity's sake, we want to focus on the word "honoring." It is the divine directive on which the fourth commandment stands firm or falls prey to sin. To honor means to uphold graciously, to submit willingly, to show respect humbly. The word *respect,* from the Latin *respectus,* means to look at or to look back on, to feel or show honor or esteem for, to show consideration. "Respect" is a good synonym for honor.

While we may not always agree with our parents, we are asked by God to honor them. We must try to appreciate the role our parents play in our becoming the persons we are called to be. Consider how Jesus submitted himself to Mary and Joseph's care for his entire hidden life. When the time came for him to preach and teach publicly, it was his submission to Mary's requests at the wedding of Cana, when she told him that the couple had no wine, that led to the performance of his first public miracle (see John 2:1-11).

FOSTERING SUBMISSION IN FAMILY SETTINGS

Family life can become a swirling sea of tension and turmoil when mutual submission and respect for the uniqueness of each member is lost. All too often the temptation arises for parents to remake their children according to their own image. Parental respect for the unique image and likeness of God in which their offspring have been created is essential to healthy family life and spiritual formation. By imposing on their children the form they want to see, parents beat their children into *conformity* rather than fostering in their offspring *co-forming* submission.

The character form God had in mind for us from the beginning can only be disclosed if we treat one another with honor and if we submit in humility to an Authority greater than ourselves. Honoring happens when parents stand back in respect and ask: "What does God have in mind for our child? What is his or her life call? Where is God leading our child, and how can we be good guides?"[1]

Children are likely to honor parents who honor them in this manner. By helping each child to realize his or her God-given destiny—and not just forcing that child to submit blindly to their will—parents find their fulfillment as well.

Parents cannot know everything about their children, nor can children know everything about their parents. Young children cannot appreciate the sacrifices each parent has to make for their benefit. Older children, too, are often oblivious to what their parents had to go through to raise them properly. Children honor their parents when they listen to their advice, enjoy their company over the years, and care for them when they are old, whether or not they live together.

HONORING DESPITE OUR ALL-TOO-HUMAN CONDITION

This commandment tells us to honor our parents, not because they are perfect people, but because by giving us life they ignited the spark of God in us. It doesn't matter if, over the years, we or they turn out to be less than God's gift to humanity! Even the ancestors of Jesus (see Matthew 1:1-17) had their shortcomings. Isaac tricked Esau into giving him his birthright (see Genesis 27:1-40). Though named a man after God's own heart, David so coveted Bathsheba that he had her husband, Uriah, killed so he could marry her (see 2 Samuel 11:1-27).

Despite their many faults and failings, human parents and their children are still honored by God. His mark within us is the mark of our distinctive humanness. Our faith teaches us that from all eternity we have been loved and embraced by the mystery of the eternal Godhead. Our most original identity, our deepest essence, lies not in biological givens but in the transcendent thrust of our spirit.[2]

When we honor our parents, as they honored their parents before them, our obedience enables God to work more freely through us. Returning to the example of Jesus, no human limits—neither of ancestry nor or of association, such as the betrayal of Judas—could thwart the plan of Holy Providence for our salvation.

We may fail to honor God in one another, but God never fails to honor us. He loves us and wants to help us, no matter where we are on this tough climb to the pinnacle of peace and joy he wants us to attain. So much does God honor us that he prepares for each of us the special graces we need to cope with the inhumanity of the very humanity he asks us to honor!

THE RISK OF SURRENDER

To honor God as Father, to submit to God's decrees, requires the risk of surrender, the courage of consent. We have to let go of preconceived plans and projects and listen, as Mary did, to a deeper call. Gabriel's announcement to her—that she would be the mother of God—was greeted with brave, unambiguous words: "Behold, I am the handmaid of the Lord. May it be done to me according to your word" (Lk 1:38). Mary's "yes" is at once bold and submissive. She trusted the Spirit totally. Her *Fiat* was not a passive giving up but an active going toward. It was not cowardly but courageous. It initiated the culminating stage of salvation history. Mary's honor was at stake, yet she did not hesitate to humble herself by consenting to the Word becoming flesh in her womb.

The fourth commandment invites us to this kind of bold submission. God has adopted us, so we belong to the family of God. We come from God, and shall one day return to God. God is our Father in another sense, too. It is he who created us, who keeps us, and who saves us through the power and love of his only begotten Son.

When we put ourselves in a similar posture of submission to a higher authority that has our best interests at heart, we do not conform blindly to a force beyond our control. Rather we seek humbly to imbibe wisdom for living. We exercise our prerogative to choose the good for the sake of serving our faith community. We obey what is commanded by God because his word is true.

Words like "may it be done to me" are risky to say. Mary did not know what the outcome would be. Neither do we. And yet God challenges us to risk such submission, to dare to say:

God of power and might, of mercy and forgiveness, I am your child. I honor you and, for your sake, the earthly parents you gave me. I do not know what you have in mind for me, but I submit in advance to your holy foreknowledge. Lead me and I will follow. Challenge me and I will change. Call me and I will go forth with confidence. Amen!

Submission of this sort brings with it an inner peace and joy not even grave disappointment can take away. As part of God's family, living under a canopy of grace and surrounded by a cloud of witnesses, we find it easier than ever to say, "Lord, here I am. Do with me what you will."

One day we may be overwhelmed with a loss so great we aren't sure if we can recover. The next day may fill us with a joy so ecstatic we don't know what we did to deserve it. The character disposition of submission enables us to "let go and let God." Our ego is no longer at the center. We are willing to turn the wheel of our life over to God, not with passive resignation but with active cooperation. We let God parent us without shirking our responsibility to parent others.

SUBMISSION AS AN AVENUE TO SPIRITUAL MATURITY

Honoring our divine Parent and our human parents in this way diffuses perfectionism. Life is not like the remote control mechanism that goes with our TV: We cannot switch the world around us off and on with the push of a button. What is, is. Our self-command is to make the best of it. Maybe the outcome will go according to our script; maybe it won't. Who knows?

One thing is certain: We are in good company when we submit, for in doing so we imitate Jesus and Mary. We follow the way of the saints. We learn from experience that self-renunciation is the portal to inner liberation.

The main message of the fourth commandment is that submission to honorable divine and human authority is an avenue to spiritual maturity. Both church and society suffer when aggressiveness and violence overpower submission and gentleness. The latter dispositions, and all that surround them, must come to the forefront of contemporary life. Only then may we see among family members as well as between strangers a softening of hatred and anger.

It may be time to submit to his authority and say to God:

I rededicate my whole life to you. I will try always to submit
to your direction. Mellow my rebellious humanity. Help me
to heed the cry to honor others in a world where dishonoring
them and denying their dignity happens daily.

If we obey this commandment, first as members of God's
family, and then as members of a human family, we can safely
say that Jesus will be born anew in our hearts and in society.
He will help us to see where we must go as the people of
God commanded to live a life of obedience. Are we not
being led from barren deserts of dishonor into the bracing air
of respect for young and old alike?

This vision of a better world begins around the family din-
ner table. Listen to one another without interruption. Honor
the divine spark in each human heart. Keep these words of
the prophet Isaiah in the forefront of your mind:

Rise up in splendor! Your light has come,
the glory of the Lord shines upon you.
See, darkness covers the earth,
and thick clouds cover the peoples;
But upon you the Lord shines,
and over you appears his glory.

Nations shall walk by your light,
and kings by your shining radiance.
Raise your eyes and look about;
they all gather and come to you:
Your sons come from afar,
and your daughters in the arms of their nurses.
Then you shall be radiant at what you see,
your heart shall throb and overflow,

For the riches of the sea shall be emptied out before you,
the wealth of nations shall be brought to you.
Caravans of camels shall fill you,
dromedaries from Midian and Ephah;
All from Sheba shall come bearing gold and frankincense,
and proclaiming the praises of the Lord.

Isaiah 60:1-6

TIME TO REFLECT ON
THE FOURTH COMMANDMENT

Step Four: Submission

In his "Letter to Families" dated February 22, 1994, Pope John Paul II said that the Church has entrusted to families the task of unleashing the forces of good—a process begun with Mary's courageous "yes" to God. To *honor* means, according to the Holy Father, to *acknowledge*: "Let yourself be guided by the firm acknowledgment of the person." This includes all members of the family, for "honor is essentially an attitude of unselfishness."[3]

In many ways, therefore, the fourth commandment addresses the need for both responsible parenting and for sensitive care of children; it teaches us to respect young and old alike. It calls us to uphold and celebrate the family of humans and the family of God.

According to *The Catechism*, the Christian family is a domestic church; a communion of persons, a sign and image of the communion of the Father and the Son in the Holy Spirit; a privileged community; and the original cell of social life [2204-2207].

By honoring our parents, we show respect not to perfect beings who provided faultless role models in our spiritual development, but to human beings who sparked the gift of God's life in us. Even when our parents' shortcomings cause us pain and emotional "baggage," by following God's command to honor them, we are freed to revel in the all-transcending, perfect fatherhood of God himself.

In "Psalm for the Nativity," composed by St. Francis of Assisi, we hear these sentiments from the heart of a loving son:

He is our most holy Father, in heaven,
and he is our King before all ages (Ps 74:12).
And he sent us his beloved Son, from on high,
to be clothed in our flesh,
born of the virgin, Mary....
On that day,
the Lord sent the gift of his mercy,
and at night his song—
an infant's cry—
was heard....
The most holy and blessed Child
was given to us!
He was born for us! (Is 9:6).
Let the heavens be glad and the earth rejoice;
let the sea and what fills it resound;
let the plains be joyful and all that is in them!
Then shall all the trees of the forest exult
before the Lord, for he comes;
for he comes to rule the earth.
He shall rule the world with justice
and the peoples with his constancy.

Psalms 96:11-13[4]

QUESTIONS FOR REFLECTION

1. Are tenderness, forgiveness, respect, fidelity, joy, peace, and mutual service the rule or the exception in our family? Do I try by word and example to teach my children how to grow in virtue, self-denial, and prudent judgment? Do I try to honor and obey my parents, not to quarrel with them constantly or neglect their needs?

Your Thoughts:

2. Do I notice a lack of nearness to God in my everyday family life? An indifference that makes it difficult, especially for children, to cultivate dispositions of the heart that result in our "honoring" one another? Do I respect the life call of my children? Do I take responsibility for their proper guidance in Christian discipleship? Do I take for granted the sacrifices my parents make for me? What can I do in the family circle to ensure that appreciation and self-donation replace ingratitude and greed?

Your Thoughts:

3. If children are unwilling or unable to serve their parents when their help is needed; if the family unit turns in upon itself and refuses to be ministers of God's saving work in this world; if its members rush around from morning to night, never pausing for shared prayer, then perhaps it is time to ask yourself what can be done *today* to change the situation. What can we do together from now on to make sure the fourth commandment does not fall into a moral vacuum?

Your Thoughts:

Honoring in Family Life

God commands us to honor those
Who gave us life with him,
To be subdued to them
As Jesus obeyed Joseph, the carpenter,
And Mary, his mother.

Family fondness may fall low
When children mature and grow:
Wearily we let them go.
Will they be caught
In fantasies wrought
By video, movie, Internet,
By gangs, by drugs that let
Their soul dry up
Till it is only an empty cup?

If they too hastily go
Toward lands of hatred, hurt, and woe,
Dishonoring us,
They may end up an easy prey
Of those who slyly say:
Clever crime does pay.

When in despair and all alone
They silently long for a loving home,
Where parents honor any child,
Mild, weak, willful, or almost wild,
Lifting them with discipline,
Not giving in to every whim.

If honoring dies in family life
It dives into a swirling pit
Of turmoil, tension, painful strife.

Honor gray-haired dad and mom,
Let them freely come
Bringing you their wistful wails,
Their endlessly repeated tales
Of ancient trials, forgotten childhood trails
Remembered in the winter
Season of their ebbing life.
Relieve the bitter cold
Of growing lonely, sick, and old.
They bend their bony shoulders
Under weighty boulders
Of years of fading dreams,
Now craving for some beams
Of saving love and light
When slowly veiled by silent night.

—Fr. Adrian van Kaam

F I V E

THE FIFTH COMMANDMENT:

"You Shall Not Kill."

The Way of Resurrection

When all these things which I have set before you, the blessings and the curses, are fulfilled in you, and from among whatever nations the Lord, your God, may have dispersed you, you ponder them in your heart: then, provided that you and your children return to the Lord, your God, and heed his voice with all your heart and all your soul, just as I now command you, the Lord, your God, will change your lot; and taking pity on you, he will again gather you from all the nations wherein he has scattered you. **Deuteronomy 30:1-3**

Just as one commandment builds upon and follows the other, so the spinal column of our character formation unfolds and strengthens with each step of the way. Our lives become more animated and creative. The sense that we are moving in a moral, ethical, and spiritual direction increases when we meet Jesus in the New Testament. He radiates adoration of the Father, veneration of his holy name, dedication to the Lord's day, and submission to the will of God in all things. He honors his foster father, Joseph, and his mother, Mary. He upholds life to such a degree that he triumphs over death.

The commandment "You shall not kill," stated positively, is an urgent summons to preserve life. God's way is not life-denying but life-affirming. It is the way of reconstruction, a celebration with Jesus of resurrection from the dead.

The stark directive offered by this fifth step to peace and joy awakens us at a time in history when murders and other violent acts of destruction have become commonplace. In the relatively safe neighborhood where we live, we were shocked to learn of a midday shooting in front of the local supermarket. A teenager was gunned down in cold blood in a gang-related homicide. People gathered at the site to mourn his death, trying to think of ways not to let the neighborhood be overrun by this kind of violent behavior.

America, "the land of the free and the home of the brave," has become a killing field. What we used to assume took place only in war zones and camps bent on ethnic cleansing is now in our backyard. Killings are on the rise every day in urban areas and small towns. The news numbs us. Terrorist bombs blast away. Firearm sales soar. A "kill or be killed" mentality grips many inner city youths, and its effects are spilling out from our city streets into the suburban areas of our country.

A life-denying nonchalance greets everything from abortion to euthanasia. Both are seen as viable options to terminate life at its weakest stages. Life becomes a commodity to be used or abused at will rather than seeing life from conception to its final passage as a precious gift of God. And yet the insidiousness of the taking of physical life pales in comparison to the far deeper character deformation it produces: the killing of the human spirit, the destruction of hope.

KILLING AS A SPIRITUAL CRISIS

Even a casual observer of the human condition can see signs of depression, lack of trust, suspicion, betrayal, and despair in people's faces. The taking of human life physically may end up destroying us spiritually. God's command not to kill protects not only the human body but the human spirit as well. Abandonment of the highest value of life produces hopelessness and despair as much as the protection of life instills assurance of the eternal and a renewal of hope. Similarly, when the human spirit cools like spent embers, when people cease to care about their most vulnerable members, physical life loses its greatest defendant.

Without the kind of God-guided character building fostered by the Ten Commandments, our bodies as well as our spirits are in danger of dying on the vine. We wonder aloud and in the stillness of our heart if the Lord of life is on our side. A spiritual crisis of this magnitude always evokes the question of whether, when all is said and done, we have been abandoned by the mystery.

This attitude attacks life where it hurts the most, in our hearts and in the maturation of our characters. It is depleting, destructive, disintegrating, and discouraging. In the face of so much death, we begin to doubt that reconstruction and resurrection to new life, to the fullness of peace and joy, is our destiny.

Yet we must believe that God's prohibition not to kill gives way to the promise of renewed hope and vitality. Though life's burdens may weigh upon us, God gives us the grace to cope with them. In every obstacle there resides an opportunity to grow into a more virtuous personality, if our faith does not falter. The darkness of death gives way to the lightness of rebirth. The life force rushes onward like a ray of sun warming our face on a cold winter's day. No event ought to be so horrendous that it kills the human spirit; in the end, resurrection always triumphs over crucifixion.

This miracle of life out of death, this movement from destruction to resurrection, was portrayed with astounding clarity on our visit to the Holocaust Museum in Washington, D.C. Exhibit after exhibit bore powerful testimony to the devastation of man's inhumanity to man. There we witnessed the wanton and arbitrary destruction of every form of creation—family life, invention, enterprise, art, and beauty. We saw photographs of whole villages that had been wiped away like chalk from school boards. The horrific evidence of it all appalled us: bloodshed, gas chambers, mass burials, vandalism, and other atrocities that nearly destroyed the Jewish people.

And yet it was in that museum that we found glimmers of hope, pockets of life and light, true resurrection moments. People of all faiths were named who had risked their lives to save even one Jewish child. Others worked tirelessly in the underground as freedom fighters in an effort to stop the carnage, even though they, too, became its victims.

When visitors shed tears, they were not only tears of grief and outrage. They were tears of admiration and hope because, as the museum so movingly reveals, life does triumph over death. That day the fifth commandment was like a clarion call rising above the din of death orchestrated by Adolf Hitler and the Nazi generals and doctors who put in motion his "final solution," the mass murder of the Jewish people. It is as if the Lord were saying to them and to us:

You shall not take away the gift of physical life I have given you. Neither shall you kill the life of the spirit. You must not do so because I, your God, am the giver of life. I am love. In my Son, Jesus, I came to give you new life and that abundantly. I am your promise of life eternal. Your body will pass away but your spirit will live forever. That is why you must not kill what is the most precious thing I have created: the human body and soul.

RECHANNELING ANGER AS LIFE-GIVERS

The fifth step to peace and joy communicates another basic goal of character unfolding: to be a life-giver. Whether we give physical life through procreation or spiritual life through inspiration, we are to become co-creators with our Creator.

Even if we are surrounded by life-deniers and nay-sayers, God wants us to be witnesses to the goodness of life wherever he places us. We must see our own and others' lives as treasures of enormous worth. With every breath we draw, we must renew our commitment not to kill. We have to profess by word and example that human life is sacred physically, psychologically, and spiritually.

Anyone who ignores this injunction and commits murder is subject to punishment in a civilized society. If human life is sacred, then to destroy or deny it is utterly unjust and even sacrilegious. The New Testament, while repeating the fifth commandment's injunction not to kill, takes it to a deeper level by adapting this divine directive to the "inner murder" of anger. Jesus, as cited in Matthew's Gospel, explains: "In the old laws it says, 'You shall not kill and whoever kills is liable to judgment'" (Mt 5:21). To this truth he adds a complementary command: "But I say to you, whoever is angry with his brother shall be liable to judgment" (Mt 5:22).

Anger is something all of us have felt. Jesus himself was enraged with justifiable anger when he chased the money-changers out of the temple. But there is another kind of anger that is capable of killing the human heart, and it, too, is liable to judgment.

Jesus warns us to rein in the destructive anger, the inner urge, that propels us at times to push others aside so that we can have our own way. It hardens our hearts to their plight. All we care about is having the upper hand. Anger can so overwhelm our best character traits that we lose self-control. Everything has to go according to our bidding. Such rage propels acts of random violence. It is as if the end justifies the means. Anger is like a rushing waterfall. At first we see white water (anger), then cascading foam (rage), then the final crash (killing).

Countering this negative, death-dealing force is God's divine, life-giving Spirit. Regardless of the form of destruction to which human life may be subjected, reconstruction through the power of the Risen Lord is always a possibility.

The fifth commandment, as expounded by Jesus, challenges us to rein in our anger and rechannel it before it becomes destructive. Psychologically, there are many therapeutic tools people can use to handle the real or imagined triggers that spark their rage. They can talk things over rationally. They can try to work out their differences. They may even resort to beating a pillow or closing themselves in a closet to shout aloud the things they would like to say to the person or persons who aroused them in this way.

These techniques may diminish the self-perpetuating force of anger, but they are inadequate when it comes to reforming our character. Jesus calls for a more radical solution. He says we have to meet force with a loving counterforce. Jesus asks us to turn the other cheek, to love our enemies, to put our sword back in its sheath, to stand for a peaceful, non-violent way of existence.

Once again, this commandment places before us two options: to choose life and its character-repleting virtues (love, mercy, peace), or death and its depleting consequences (murder, violence, rage). There can only be one choice for us: the light must continue to shine. The resurrection must be proclaimed and lived in all its fullness, for if life has no higher meaning and purpose, then one value after another will fall, releasing the barbaric. To offset this destructive mentality, we fervently pray:

> *Lord Jesus, wherever death roams in our world, have mercy on the dying. Upon anyone facing their final hour, bestow the shining light of your mercy. Let your light and your risen life be for others a beam of uplifting hope. Help us never to succumb to demonic forces that are death-dealing and life-denying, parasites that breed the soul-sicknesses of discouragement and despair. Give us the good medicine of trust and appreciative abandonment to the mystery. Lord, be with us as we choose to celebrate life.*

Such prayers of the heart show the power of the Decalogue to direct our motivations and moral choices. In the light of the fifth commandment, we pray for the grace to attend solicitously to the overall well-being of ourselves (Have we truly chosen life?) and of others (Do they see us as life-givers?).

REPERCUSSIONS OF VIRTUOUS
CHARACTER FORMATION

Because human beings are called from the beginning "to share, by knowledge and love, in God's own life" [*The Catechism*, 356], it follows that not only is God living in each of us; he has through his Son, Jesus Christ, given us a second chance to attain life eternal. Our hope of resurrection wipes away the fear of death. Through the power of the Risen Lord, reconstruction of soul is always a possibility, regardless of the destruction to which it has been exposed.

Several African missionaries, attending our formation sessions in Pittsburgh, confirmed our observation that when people who have known persecution and impoverishment convert to Christianity, their whole appearance changes. They become radiant, happy, vital, and full of hope. The good news of the resurrection of Jesus is mirrored in their eyes and facial expressions. It may be because they feel overwhelmed with joy by the revelation that God loves us so much that he gave his only Son to save us.

Where a transcendent outlook prevails, there life can be found. No wonder in countries like Africa hundreds of people are baptized every year, churches are filled with worshipers, and seminary as well as religious life flourishes.

People come to the waters of Baptism because they seek a way to make sense of the mystery of life and death. They know intuitively that character formation in virtue presupposes an innate understanding of right and wrong, of the difference between good and evil, blessedness and conflict. What they seek is communion with the Risen Christ, for whom death is not the end but the beginning of new life.

Picture a baby girl coming to term in the womb of her mother. She feels protected, warm, fed, and surrounded by a quiet, life-sustaining environment. Then comes the great day of birth. Catapulted from an embryonic environment into a harsh world with glaring lights and a definite wake-up call must be a real shock! The baby wails. She isn't happy at all.

This story repeats itself as we grow up. We live in the temporary womb of daily life. Afraid of dying, we know life will end someday. What happens then may not be so different from birth. One way ends, another begins. We come into the full glory, the full light, of the heavenly Jerusalem.

Death, when it is allowed to occur in God's time, is like birth in that it has a great lesson to teach. If on earth we do not gain insight into the real purpose of our being, we risk experiencing a lost life, a deflated sense of a higher destiny.

If life has no meaning beyond making money and looking important, it may end in ego-desperation. The futility of it all may be overwhelming. The highest rate of suicide among professionals appears to be among psychiatrists. Here are people who deal with life's peaks and valleys, though some of them seem to be unaware of its ultimate meaning.

No wonder the fifth commandment begs for a new hearing. It is as if the Lord is saying, *"Don't kill yourself or anyone. Life is worth living if only you will place your trust in me."*

At the center of this circle of forming, reforming, and transforming love is God himself. He attends to every detail in creation. Not a sparrow falls from the air nor a hair from our head without his knowing it (see Matthew 10:29-31). Without him we have nothing. Nothing money can buy has any meaning, at the core of our character, we feel empty. To live an anti-God life, which is to say an anti-Gospel life, is to forfeit our best chances for peace and joy. Before long, paradoxes like the cross and the resurrection, joy in suffering, and wealth in poverty make no sense at all.

WORDS THAT KILL

We violate the fifth commandment not only by killing life but by causing suffering to the human spirit. We can manage to kill joy in ourselves and others. It is as if our own inner life is chronically suicidal. And, were this not bad enough, we drive others to the suicide of their dreams, hopes, ideals, and enthusiasms. We become killers by using insulting language to crush children's confidence, often under the guise of rigid religiosity and pseudo-spirituality. We scoff at the handicapped and people who try to better themselves; we shirk any form of responsibility. It is as if a black cloud surrounds us. When we enter a room, the atmosphere changes.

This "killer" mentality hurts people emotionally. It abuses them in mind and soul, and can affect them bodily, as studies of anorexia and other eating disorders show. Spiritual murder can be lastingly detrimental. It smashes the initial formation in childhood, which are the building blocks that shape virtuous character in adulthood. This commandment forbids the killing of innocent spirits, yet some parents say things that shake their confidence:

"Shut up!"

"You're nothing but a brat!"

"I wish you were never born!"

"Drop dead."

"You'll put a nail in my coffin."

By acting as though their children were annoyances rather than gifts, parents can kill life at its most vulnerable stages. Remorse may set in at a later date, but the damage has already been done.

People may destroy life spiritually not because they premeditate their actions but because they are enraged by their own loss of meaning. Blind jealousy, mindless beatings, and date rapes are acts of spontaneous combustion that destroy everything in their wake.

To test the depth of our obedience to this commandment, each of us must ask:

Am I a life-giving person? Am I appreciative of every facet of creation? Do I feel compassion for the suffering no human escapes? Am I a Christian in name only, or am I becoming one in spirit with the dying and rising of my Lord? Do I distort the words of Holy Scripture or the exhortations of the spiritual masters by taking them out of context and using them to kill the spirit of hope, joy, and profound appreciation in people?

It is wonderful to see how life blossoms in a loving family. Where love is, life abounds. Whether we witness love between newlyweds or wordless exchanges between old couples, our spirits rise. We blossom in an atmosphere where kindness, gentleness, and joy prevail.

The words of the prophet Jeremiah help us to understand how much God values our life: "Before I formed you in the womb I knew you, and before you were born I dedicated you" (Jer 1:5). God designed life to be a consecration, not a desecration. To kill is always in a sense to commit "deicide," for we are taking the life of something or someone God has created. We are destroying a human heart divinely illumined with sparks of daring dreams for the kingdom.

In God's eyes, everything about us is holy—from newborn toe prints to frail and aged fingers, from our first words to our mature ideas. God continues to breathe new life into us. Even in our suffering, his presence sustains us:

"I will never desert you. I will be with you in this life and prepare you for the next. You may cry when you leave the earth as you cried when you entered it. But I am preparing for you a better place. Be not afraid."

BECOMING LIFE-GIVERS

A corollary to the fifth commandment is the necessity of caring for the physical health and social well-being of others. It is not enough that we avoid murder; we must care for the people around us who are in need of food, clothing, shelter, and health care.

In creating a climate that respects life, we live in imitation of the Lord of life. He provided hungry people with both earthly food (fish and bread) and heavenly food (his own body and blood). At first they found it impossible to believe he was the Messiah. Whether he taught in a synagogue or in an open field, listeners were stunned by the wisdom of his words, by the gentle yet firm way in which he expressed the truth. They saw alive in him the love of God. Everything about him revealed how good life could be if one lived by the commandments.

Christianity is not a gospel of gloom; it is good news. It does not deny the suffering we cannot escape; it shows us the hope of the resurrection. Already in the temporal sphere, Jesus wants us to taste the eternal.

In the light of the resurrection, the sacrifices life asks of us gain new significance. They are stopping places *and* starting points on our faith and formation journey. They are teachable moments, increasing our understanding of the commandments. As to the fifth, what it forbids is killing; what it forecasts is the basic peace and joy that will be ours if we live in obedience to the Lord, who says of himself: "I am the resurrection and the life; whoever believes in me, even if he dies, will live and everyone who lives and believes in me will never die" (Jn 11:25-26). He made the choice Yaweh set before us in the Book of Deuteronomy, for these oft quoted words convey remarkable power in the context of the fifth commandment:

> Here, then, I have today set before you life and prosperity, death and doom. If you obey the commandments of the Lord, your God, which I enjoin on you today, loving him, and walking in his ways, and keeping his commandments, statutes, and decrees, you will live and grow numerous, and the Lord, your God, will bless you in the land that you are entering to occupy.... I call heaven and earth today to witness against you. I have set before you life and death, the blessing and the curse. Choose life, then, that you and your descendants may live, by loving the Lord, your God, heeding his voice, and holding fast to him.
>
> **Deuteronomy 30:15-20**

This choice, rightly made, is vividly portrayed in a true story told by John Killinger.[1] Two young missionaries, Jim and Elisabeth, went to minister to the Auca Indians of Ecuador, an extremely primitive tribe. Jim and four other young men flew into Auca territory. They dropped gifts and messages in the language of the people, assuring them of their love and good will. As soon as their aircraft had landed on a strip of sand by the river, the Indians greeted them, not with hospitality but with lances. All the men were killed.

This was not the end of the story, however. Three years

later their wives had returned to Ecuador. They had learned the Auca language but, instead of trying to convict the people, they simply waited for their welcome. Elisabeth sat in a thatched hut a few miles from the beach where Jim and the others had been slain. With her were two of the seven tribesmen who had murdered the missionary party.

Eventually the Auca women invited the missionary wives to live among them. The men had killed the missionaries because they feared that the missionaries were themselves killers. The Aucas did not know that they had come bearing gifts. They thought they had come to dominate and destroy the tribe. Now love overcame mutual fear. A people, far away from civilization as we know it, found new life thanks to the love of Jesus. They found his love in these self-giving and forgiving women, who were living witnesses to the resurrection. Their characters were truly Christ-formed.

Killinger then offers us this challenge. If we can't do something in Christ's name, why should we do it at all?[2] If we can't be life-givers, why pretend that we believe in the resurrection? Inspired by the Book of Deuteronomy and pledged to obey this commandment, we pray:

May the Lord of life pitch his tent in our heart. May he surround us with the warmth of love, the sweetness of hope, the conviction of faith. May we always be givers of life, not killers of peace and joy. Then the Lord will bless our days on earth until we, too, shall know in eternity the splendor of his risen glory. We shall never perish but rest in peace. Amen.

TIME TO REFLECT ON
THE FIFTH COMMANDMENT

Step Five: Resurrection

In commanding us not to kill, our Lord challenged us to protect life, especially at its most vulnerable stages. He denounced anger and hatred as immoral. We are to oversee with his help the well-being of life socially, physically, emotionally, and spiritually. Our reward will be the gift of a happy life and a healthy soul, not only now but for eternity. We experience in the light of God's promise peace in our heart and joy in our world.

Peace is not merely the absence of war; it is the work of justice and the effect of charity. While allowing for legitimate defense and just punishment,[3] the fifth commandment moves us to do all that we can to prevent the causes of war and its death-dealing effects by creating just conditions to foster decent standards of living and deterring aggressors. Given the weaponry at hand in our world, including nuclear forces capable of unleashing massive destruction, obeying the fifth commandment becomes a survival imperative of the twenty-first century.

Years ago, in the sixteenth century, the reformer Martin Luther wrote words we would do well to heed today:

God... wants us to keep this commandment ever before our eyes as a mirror in which we see ourselves, so that we may be attentive to his will and with hearty confidence and prayer commit to him whatever wrong we suffer.... Thus we may learn to calm our anger and have a patient, gentle heart, especially toward those who have given us occasion for anger, namely, our enemies.[4]

This step to peace and joy also includes a commitment not to give scandal, which is to say, not to kill the spirit of trust in people who have put their faith in us; not to establish laws or social structures leading to the decline of morals and the corruption of religious practice, or, in the words of *The Catechism*, not to "intentionally or not, make Christian conduct and obedience to the Commandments difficult and practically impossible" [2286].

As with every commandment, the fifth commandment offers both prohibition and promise. In this commandment, we are not only directed not to kill; we are called to become life-givers. Thus business leaders who incite others to commit fraud, teachers who provoke their pupils to anger, and those who tear down the moral values of others are all guilty of disobeying this commandment.

Life-givers embrace the virtue of temperance, and respect both human dignity and bodily integrity. They avoid every kind of excess, from the abuse of food to the endangerment of life due to speeding or other carelessness. This commandment forbids such hostile acts as kidnaping and hostage taking to forced sterilization or mutilation. By implication, it commands us to respect the dead, and to prepare the dying to meet their God. In so doing, we proclaim our faith in the resurrection and our hope in life everlasting.[5]

QUESTIONS FOR REFLECTION

1. Do I understand that this commandment is more than an order to refrain from killing? That it is a call to give life, to be channels of grace, to answer to hate and derision, as Jesus did, with love and forgiveness?

Your Thoughts:

2. What must I do to renew my commitment to protect life from the moment of conception to the moment of natural death? Do I understand that killing is destructive not only physically, but psychologically and spiritually as well?

Your Thoughts:

3. Have I allowed a spirit of death to enter my heart by harboring unforgiveness or hatred? What can I do to temper aggression instead of being ruled by it? To catch and control hidden hostility disguised as a zeal for righteousness? To transform a world of warriors into a land of life-givers and true lovers? To spread the gift of peace to all corners of the earth so that we may be worthy to be called children of God (see Matthew 5:9)?

Your Thoughts:

Command to Honor Humankind

At-oneness with the Lord,
Faith in his Eternal Word,
Commands us to honor humankind.
What shocks heart and mind
Is wanton killing worldwide.
The slaying of the innocent who went
Into the killing fields and weeds,
The backyards of our teeming streets.

Teenagers destroy each other wantonly.
Numbed, we bend our knee,
Beseeching Thee to stop the slaying
Of youngsters who as kids were praying
In our little church and humble home.
Please save them, leave them not alone.

Hear the piercing wails
Of mothers, fathers, children.
Behold the sticky, oozing trails
From beloved bodies.
Heal the anarchy loosed in humanity.
Rekindle the dying love embers of our race,
No longer do we see your loving face.

Rekindle light in doubting minds,
Darkened by the pains of time.
Let us unwind and patiently await
The brightness of a life of faith
That the dead shall rise victoriously.

Instill in us your clarion call:
"You shall not kill."
Turn us into a resurrection power
Which should flower when we are caught
In a course of violent pulsations.
Don't let us drown in their pent-up rage, lest
A treacherous hurricane, a thundering waterfall
In the end may cover all.

White waters of anger
Gain in power,
Gathering devastating energy
Till a cascading rage
Takes center stage:
Wild thunders the final crash of callous killing,
Killing blinds all wise willing
Of what is commanded by our God.

Put your dangerous swords, without bitter words,
Shining, back in their sheaths.
Replace bellicosity with blessedness,
Desecration of life with consecration.
Don't diminish the splendor of any liveliness
By discouraging depreciation instead
    of animation.
Be a new lease on life, not a limit on my power
That inspires life and makes you flower.

—Fr. Adrian van Kaam

SIX

THE SIXTH COMMANDMENT:

"You Shall Not Commit Adultery."

The Way of Confirmation

Lord, God of Abraham, Isaac, and Israel, let it be known this day that you are God in Israel and that I am your servant and have done all these things by your command. **1 Kings 18:36**

Crafting or forming our character, as we have seen, is a step-by-step process traceable in the teachings of the Ten Commandments. These directives support what is right morally, just as, to repeat our analogy, our spinal column holds us upright physically and enables us to stand on two feet. The commandments are the backbone of the life of the Spirit. No happiness of life or health of soul is possible unless we obey them. The prohibitions inherent in these ways are also invitations to develop a character modeled on the moral fiber of our Judeo-Christian faith and formation tradition.

The sixth commandment contains a wealth of insight about the meaning of love and its responsible expression. In a culture where infidelity abounds, where it is predicted that one out of two marriages will end in divorce, we know it is not easy to love either faithfully or responsibly. Yet this is our God-given call. We are to love one another as God has loved us.

Whether we are single or married, the commandment is the same. We are equally responsible before God to bestow chastely and to receive gratefully the gift of love. Fidelity may seem to be an impossible ideal amidst a media blitz bound to the pleasure principle, but it must be our goal.

The prohibition of this commandment (which forbids us to violate the trust of those we love) also holds out to us a promise. It is as if the Lord is saying to us:

To love as I have called you to love means that you must emulate my fidelity. True love is never unfaithful or fickle. It is both responsible and fruitful.

Every human being I created longs for this kind of love. Alas, many may not know the source of their yearning. They will feel at times, as my Son did, the terrible pain of loneliness. Their desire for oneness with me can be misdirected. When temptation comes, listen to my commandment. It will help you to love in a more faithful, compassionate, joyful, and committed way.

Fidelity is the avenue to freedom. Infidelity is a dead-end street. It burdens your heart with guilt, a weight harder to bear than any amount of solitude.

Spiritual guilt, the guilt that compels your spirit to conform to my commandments, leads you home to me. Lacking a commitment to keep my word will carry you far away from the peace and joy you seek. Do not be anxious or afraid. I will help you to get past this danger point of misdirection and self-deception.

Because of sin, you may feel as if you have lost my love and mercy. Nothing could be farther from the truth. The greater the sinner, the greater is his or her claim on my forgiveness.

I am a faithful God. Despite your sinfulness I seek your companionship. I want you to love me as I love you. I want you to live up to your potential to be faithful lovers in an unfaithful world. One of the ways you can do so is by developing a character that protects love from the wounds inflicted by adultery. Your willingness to be faithful to my way of loving is essential.

Never hurt another human being by breaking your promise. Never reduce him or her to an object of your desire. Do not forfeit their trust for a cheap tryst. My way of loving is self-giving and other-centered. It is the model to follow. That is why I forbid you to commit adultery.

THE PAIN OF INFIDELITY

On this sixth step to peace and joy, the Lord asks us to think about the deeper meaning of trust and its opposite, betrayal or distrust. This dilemma is portrayed vividly in the life of Jesus. When he called the twelve, he trusted them to follow him. He must have wondered if their lives could be reformed to conform to his way of loving. They were all so different. He even allowed Judas into the original circle of the twelve. Jesus gave him every chance to prove himself, but when he needed his loyalty the most, Judas betrayed him with a kiss (see Luke 22:48). The Master must have felt something of the pain a woman or man feels when they know their most trusted other is a betrayer, too.

Adultery hurts. It shatters trust, evokes guilt, and severs friendship. The pain is intense. This is the kind of hurt Jesus felt. We need him to help us to get through these tragic times. They are tough, but they can be transforming.

Infidelity blocks spiritual maturity and retards character formation. It can make us bitter, kill joy, and destroy peace, or it can serve as a call to forgiveness and reconciliation. Some may choose the lonely route of noninvolvement since they cannot bear to be hurt again. Others may be graced with the light of a transformed relationship.

The call to fidelity in marriage as well as in the single life is as countercultural as the teaching of all Ten Commandments. In a world that accepts so matter-of-factly a divorce mentality, why not commit adultery? Watching the "soaps" every day, people learn immoral, if not amoral, ways of relating. Cheating becomes something "everyone" does out of boredom. The teachings of Holy Scripture may or may not be able to press past the dehumanizing trends set by such media.

In a "feel good," self-centered culture, it is mandatory for us to heal our hearts and learn to love others as Jesus loves us. We cannot do so alone. We need not only the Lord's guidance but also the support of a faith community to practice the kind of love that is responsible, faithful, forgiving, and true. Adultery, terrible as it is, might shock people into starting the journey to spiritual maturity. Thus we pray:

Faithful God, as we learn to imprint these Ten Command-ments on our hearts, we remember your promise to be beside us during the fiercest storms, when raw emotions churn the sea around us and threaten to drown us. Knowing our weakness in the realm of the senses, we ask you for the grace to respect our sexuality as an expression of our spirituality.

The world fights us on this score. It preaches sex apart from responsible, respectful love in marriage. To remain faithful to a spouse, to be a true friend or an honest single person, requires a strength and a perseverance that are quite beyond us.

Merciful Lord, we ask you to fill the lonely spaces in our life. Quell our doubts and misgivings with the felt awareness of your intimacy. You know us through and through. You love us. You are Emmanuel, God-with-us. Be the Divine Physician who binds our wounds. Heal those places in us that still burn with the pain of misguided emotions. Show us the far horizons of forgiveness. Grant us the grace to make a new start. Help us to follow the way to fidelity and freedom, which you teach us.

Imprint on our hearts the disposition to confirm in one another the splendor of a fully human love. Bless women who bear children and the husbands who support them. Give both parents the courage to bring children into this world and the wisdom to guide their growth. Help us to become people who imitate your love. Give us Christ-formed characters and the backbone we need to live the commandments.

THE GIFT OF CONFORMING FIDELITY

Any relationship between spouses or in a community setting among friends is an expression of a far more profound intimacy between God and us. It follows, then, that we cannot affirm others unless we feel affirmed by God.

Jesus shows us that no love is greater than that by which one friend lays down his or her life for another (see John 15:13). Love does not grow in a safety zone of fearful withdrawal. It requires us to take the risk, as Jesus did, to love without limit despite the possibility of betrayal. Worse than any human betrayal is a break with God. We must accept his offer to repent and seek reconciliation. There is no use settling for less when God calls us to so much more.

Sooner or later, it may come to pass that even the best marriages or the best friendships or the best forms of community life still leave something to be desired. A mark of spiritual maturity is our willingness to give one another the benefit of the doubt, to trust our good intentions insofar as possible, without expecting perfection. It is a confirmation of our faith when we can say:

Thank you, Lord, for this wife or husband of mine, for this blessed friendship, for this supportive community, despite their faults. When I feel alone, misunderstood, without support, open the ears of my heart so I can hear your patient and persistent call. Help me to answer it with a resounding "Here I am." Do not let sin weaken my will and tie my tongue. When I try to satisfy this longing for you in ignoble relationships, expose my foolish ways and by your grace turn me around. For no love but yours can ever be wholly satisfying.

If we seek final confirmation of our faith in anyone or anything less than in God, we will never find it. It may be tempting to seek perfection in a partner, a friend, a community. We begin to dream about what could be. We fail to see the limited yet lovely gift of this face, this house, this neighborhood. As our appreciation increases, so does our ability to confirm the goodness we find everywhere.

Painful times can become formation opportunities, challenges to change what can be changed while accepting life's uncontrollable limits. What counts is uniting ourselves faithfully to the loving will of God. Though slogans may suggest that the grass is always greener on the other side, what counts for God is our response to the here and now.

The only way to resist the temptation to infidelity is to root our single life or our marriage in the rich soil of God's confirming love. None of this world's fleeting pleasures can make us happy if we exclude the "more than." Why fool ourselves on this score?

Though Jesus forgave the woman caught in adultery, and in this confirmed her good will, he told her emphatically to go and sin no more (see John 8:11). She had to make something of her life. She was worth more than any demeaning affair. We do not know what happened to her after her encounter with the Lord, but we can hope that she became more cognizant of life's limits, more available to the graces she needed to resist temptation.

Accepting the grace of divine confirmation is the best antidote to self-absorption. It guarantees that we will not be so concerned about our own cares that we refuse to listen to a lonely child, an insecure friend, or a lifelong companion who feels taken for granted.

CHASTENING OUR LOVE
THROUGH COMMITTED RELATIONSHIPS

This commandment gives us a definite *not*, but it also contains several *oughts*. We ought to treasure as God's own gifts our family members and friends. We ought to appreciate the blessed relationships that fill our life rather than focusing on what we might have missed.

Chaste, respectful love offers more confirmation than almost any other disposition. It is a hallmark of human freedom, a virtue needed as much in marriage as in the single life. Chastening our relationships, like an apprenticeship in self-mastery, trains us in the art and discipline of withholding gratification for the sake of a greater good.

To listen simultaneously to the demands of chastity and the choices we must make for God's sake is not easy in a culture that flaunts "free love." If we buy into the lie, our irresponsible behavior only entraps us more. Faced by the irrefutable evidence of sexually transmitted diseases and teenage pregnancies, society is coming to realize what God has been telling us all along: Our deeds and desires have consequences for which we are responsible.

Instead of emptying their hearts in uncommitted relationships, men and women called to marriage are to seek the solidity of a monogamous relationship protected by what the sixth commandment prohibits. This difficult yet delightful step to peace and joy can only be ascended if one cultivates a deep friendship and intimacy with God while one is single. The hunger of our hearts is first and foremost a hunger for God, for a person-to-Person friendship with him that lasts. This divine love is the only basis for any truly satisfying experience of human love.

Loving as Jesus loved is the work of a lifetime. It means being faithful and true to our word. It calls for a willingness on our part to bind together what has been fractured by falsehood and, above all, to make only those promises we intend to keep.

We once met a Navy chaplain, a Protestant minister, whose story reveals the everyday struggle that following this commandment entails. Deployed for nine months on an aircraft carrier, he came face-to-face with the hardship of adhering to his commitment to fidelity every time his ship docked in a foreign port. Countless were the times he could have cheated on his wife and "gotten away with it." We asked him how he maintained love for his spouse and loyalty to her under the circumstances.

The chaplain admitted that there was no easy answer to this question. Willpower alone would not have been enough, though that was important. First he had to make the effort, in the context of prayer, to turn the pain of loneliness associated with missing her into the joy of his and her solitude before God. Then they could be together in a spirit-to-spirit bond. What the sailors under his care experienced when they left the ship and went ashore was often the opposite. The only thing many could think of doing was to relieve their loneliness through alcohol and sex.

At the same time, there were others on the ship who were fighting the same battle as he, so much so that he made the ideals of chaste love and commitment as married or single persons the leading themes of his ministry. He taught the troops what it meant to be faithful. He assured them that a life of deeper intimacy with God, as they knew him, would help them more than anything else when temptation struck. A few accepted his invitation to learn and practice a form of contemplative prayer. They soon found it was the only thing that kept them going. "If it hadn't been for Scripture and spiritual reading, for prayer and a sense of service," he told us, "all I believed in might have been lost."

Then the chaplain went on to relate the story of what really saved his marriage, an unforgettable event of grace. It was late at night. His day had been tiring. He needed some fresh air. So he climbed to the top deck of the aircraft carrier and stood for a while looking up at the vast sky filled with stars.

What happened next touched him profoundly. As he allowed himself to feel his loneliness, he asked Jesus to come down from the heavens and embrace him under the starry sky. He knew that the same Lord who was holding him was holding his wife and that they were somehow together in that divine embrace. At that moment, so filled was he with peace and joy that nothing, certainly not a little fling in some port of call, could compare with this awesome experience of intimacy with God. He knew then that he could lift their mutual love to God. Jesus himself would seal the bond that held them together.

The chaplain confirmed our belief that a character formed in the virtue of chaste, respectful love is solid as a rock. That is why the sixth commandment can be read as a clarion call to purify our intentions, for we are always in danger of falling. Loving chastely is a mark of grace that makes us distinctively human.

OVERCOMING LUST

In the culture of Jesus' time, women were bought and sold like cattle. If a woman was caught in adultery, she was the one who got stoned, yet men might do the same and get away with it. No one challenged the Master—in fact they all walked away—when he said in front of the woman caught in adultery, "Let the one among you who is without sin be the first to throw a stone at her" (Jn 8:7). No one did. Many of these men may themselves have felt lust for her.

In Matthew's Gospel, Jesus spells out the difference between love and lust. He repeats the commandment, "You have heard that it was said, 'You shall not commit adultery'" (Mt 5:27). He then adds a startling new insight. "Everyone who looks at a woman with lust has already committed adultery with her in his heart" (Mt 5:28).

In an argument with the Pharisees on the topic of marriage and divorce, Jesus was equally emphatic: "He said to them, 'Whoever divorces his wife and marries another commits adultery against her; and if she divorces her husband and marries another, she commits adultery'" (Mk 10:11-12).

These are not easy texts to hear in a soap-opera world where marriage is no deterrent to adultery, but Jesus is not one to mince words. He helps us to see that what really counts in God's eyes is our maturation in virtue, not doing what we want with no concern for others. The question is: Are we willing to overcome the sins and vices associated with lust and unchastened love that coat our heart like sticky tar, making it impossible for us to move toward true intimacy?

The Apostle James refers to the assembly he is addressing in his letters, because of their transgressions against the law, as adulterers (see James 2:11). By this he means that to love the world in its worldly ways is to commit a kind of adultery against God. To replace our confirmation by him with lustful adherence to lower forms of power, pleasure, and possession is to play the role of a harlot where God is concerned. Yet despite this enmity, God beckons us to a deeper unity. He seeks us in our deserts of loss and invites us home to him.

John Killinger writes at length about this commandment. He wonders at a certain point in his reflections why adultery cuts so deep. As he sees it, the adulterer says in effect, "I no longer truly value our relationship. My own desires are more important than our love."[1]

He then links the sixth commandment to the fifth, not to kill, and to the seventh, not to steal. Killinger observes that all three commandments forbid taking what does not belong to us: another's life, another's wife, and another's valuables. Adultery breaks binding promises. It kills faith. It steals trust.

People battle with lust every day. Some have tried to regulate its power through legislation—laws against pornography, for example. But such laws are of only limited use; they can effect no real change unless accompanied by conversion of heart. A person can tell him or herself not to do something, but as we have seen, it takes more than willpower to resist temptation. It takes a love relationship with God and a sense of divine confirmation.

Whatever addiction we must break, be it to a substance like drugs or alcohol, or to a sexually recurrent act like solicited sex or masturbation, the freedom not to do it has to come from the free choice to do what God asks of us. We see that life has a higher purpose than pleasure.

LEARNING TO LOVE OTHERS AS GOD LOVES US

As we begin to open up to God in heartfelt prayer, as we grow in intimacy with others and ask for forgiveness, reformation gives way to transformation. Our life changes. We begin to see beyond the stars, as did the chaplain who walked that night on the deck of the aircraft carrier, to the eternal reaches of time. He looked up and saw not only points of light but the presence of God. He felt divine confirmation and the courage to live his convictions.

This hold on him by a loving God is what enabled him to hold on to his pledge to remain faithful to his spouse. When he preached on the beatitude, "Blessed are the pure of heart, for they shall see God," everyone listening knew he was speaking from experience.

There is no more powerful deterrent to adultery in marriage or in myriad small infidelities than to see God in his fidelity to us and to seek his intimacy. It is the start of a life-long process of reconciliation, of being given the chance to reform a perhaps hitherto deformed character.

According to John Killinger, "Lust and adultery have to do with self-will, with the gratification of impulses that are merely physical. Peace and joy come from doing God's will. When God rules our hearts, when God alone is supreme, we will and we can resist temptation. When the soul is filled with God, it has no room for adulterous thoughts."[2]

TIME TO REFLECT ON
THE SIXTH COMMANDMENT

Step Six: Confirmation

Both the married and single expressions of love are shadows of the perfect love of God. Both kinds of love require a single-hearted devotion and an unwavering discipline. Both require a strength that can only be obtained from God.

It is impossible to understand the prohibition against adultery without considering the call to chastity. *The Catechism* says in this regard:

> Chastity means the successful integration of sexuality within the person and thus the inner unity of man in his bodily and spiritual being.... Chastity includes an *apprenticeship in self-mastery* which is a training in human freedom.... "Indeed [in the words of St. Augustine] it is through chastity that we are gathered together and led back to the unity from which we were fragmented into multiplicity" [2337-2340][3]

This commandment reminds us that God, who created us, male and female in his own image (see Genesis 1:26-27; Mark 10:6), inscribed in the humanity of man and woman the vocation, and thus the capacity and responsibility, of love and communion.[4]

The sixth commandment reminds us that our sexuality affects all aspects of who we are in body, mind, and soul. It concerns what we must do, whether we are single or married, to remain faithful to Christ's way of chaste, respectful love. It includes how we actualize our capacity to love in the gift of procreation in marriage and in the aptitude to form bonds of communion and community in family life and friendships. The prohibition of adultery thus implies the promise that we will learn the meaning of respectful, responsible love.

QUESTIONS FOR REFLECTION

1. Since chaste, respectful love does not happen easily or automatically, how can I encourage self-control, especially in adolescents, when the vital and passionate dimension of their personality is strongly emerging? How should I address the problems of sexual abuse, child pornography, and teenage pregnancy?

Your Thoughts:

2. What can I do in my own home and in society to protect and uphold the promise of fidelity two people pledge to one another when they marry? Do I believe that the *yes* married people say to one another implies without compromise a *no* to infidelity? Do I recognize and resist the obstacles to committed love, as stated in *The Catechism: lust* (morally disordered sexual pleasure sought for itself); *masturbation* ("an intrinsically and gravely disordered

action"); *fornication* (carnal union between the unmarried); *pornography* (which perverts the conjugal act); *prostitution* (which reduces the person to an instrument of sexual pleasure); *rape* ("the forcible violation of the sexual intimacy of another person")? [2351-2356].

Your Thoughts:

3. Is friendship with Christ in a person-to-Person love relationship, one in which he becomes my all-in-All, my first order of concern, regardless of my marital status? Since friendship with and in Christ leads to spiritual bonding, to a true I-Thou interchange, how can I make this Christ-centered intimacy the source of what strengthens me to remain faithful to my life call as a single or a married person?

Your Thoughts:

Demands of Endless Love

O blessed purity,
Descending from divinity,
Decorating personhood
With the virginal wood of virtues,
Inviting home the lost and lonely dove
Of selfless love, key to serenity,
To loving compassionately,
To mirroring the Trinity.

Clouds of loneliness darken the soul
Yearning for a home in you alone.
Graces descend without end,
Amazing amounts I cannot count.
They command faithfulness in love.
Be a faithful lover in a faithless land
That banned the great command.

Betrayal of love,
A poison infecting a heart unsuspecting,
The shattering of trust by the longings of lust.
Creeping erosion of faith and fiber
In old and young, all creeds and races.
Fill the spaces in lonely hearts,
Aching painfully for your mystery.

Do not hide from temptation
In safety zones of isolation.
Risk love despite the threat
Of love betrayed.

Eternal Father,
Tenderly gather scattered lives
Around the lighthouse of your commands,
Demands of your care, your endless love.
Rescue ships oft broken
In tempests of illusion.
Explode the lie that love is license,
Elusive bird, singing seductively,
Bringing no peace, no lasting joy.
Love dies with this bird in brief embrace
Behind the bars of its confining cage.

—Fr. Adrian van Kaam

S E V E N

THE SEVENTH COMMANDMENT:

"You Shall Not Steal."

The Way of Restitution

But if a wicked man, turning from the wickedness he has committed, does what is right and just, he shall preserve his life; since he has turned away from all sins which he committed, he shall surely live, he shall not die. **Ezekiel 18:27-28**

The seventh commandment marks a turning point in the work of character formation. Its focus is not only on our connection to people and events but also to things. The God of justice, peace, and mercy invites us to respect property owned by others. This respect dignifies our own and their personhood. What are the repercussions of this step to virtuous living in community?

Many of us, being of good will, might feel exonerated from the prohibition to steal. Most people reading this book would not willfully take things that belong to others any more than they would kill or commit adultery.

If the commandments were only meant by God for so-called criminal types, we might be inclined to doubt their basic truth. The point is, they were given to a group of people called the "Chosen," not to a band of outlaws.

Yahweh proclaimed his demands to women and men selected to enter into a covenant with him—a people from whose line in the fullness of time the Word Made Flesh would come among us.

God entrusted to his people a way of life designed to lead them to lasting peace and joy, on the condition that they made the effort to craft their character in accordance with his word. Even though they were his "Chosen," it stands to reason that there were some among them who thought nothing of stealing. Poor populations often had a kind of Robin Hood mentality. They assumed that stealing from the rich to give to the poor could be done with impunity. But this commandment, as much as the other nine, is unambiguous; its prohibition is clear. Whether one is guilty of petty thievery or bank robbery, God forbids us to steal. The question is: How does stealing damage character building in virtue and why does restitution restore us to favor with God?

DEGENERATIVE EFFECTS OF STEALING

Let's begin with so-called childish examples of candy-swiping or stealing from another student's homework. Are these merely innocent acts? Or do they pave the way for greater evils in adulthood? Our conviction is that sinful habits, unchecked in childhood, have degenerative effects on character development as one matures. It becomes easier to take things that do not belong to us and feel no remorse, let alone feeling obliged to make restitution. Yet we know from Scripture that virtue has to be consistent: as the child, so the man.

Recall how Jesus blessed Zacchaeus for his faith and his pledge: "Behold, half of my possessions, Lord, I shall give to the poor, and if I have extorted anything from anyone I shall repay it four times over" (Lk 19:8). It strikes us that Zacchaeus must have had a solid, moral upbringing by God-fearing parents to feel this way later in life. As a tax collector, he had wealth, but that was not enough to satisfy his heart's search for life's deeper meaning. That quest sparked in him a longing to see Jesus. Jesus in turn saw in Zacchaeus real goodness. Here was a man who would repent, were he ever in the least way to disobey the seventh commandment. Visibly impressed, Jesus said to Zacchaeus that salvation had come to him, a descendent of Abraham (see Luke 19:9).

Stealing not only erodes virtue in us; it offends the just order of society. That is why this commandment demands that one make restitution in kind for what one has stolen, for stealing is a violation of another's right to ownership and a diminishment of respect for his or her dignity. Anyone who has ever been robbed feels violated not only because of what is missing but because of a gross invasion of his or her privacy. Trust deteriorates. Suspicion becomes second nature.

Mental and spiritual deterioration are two serious consequences of violating the seventh commandment. This command prohibits other, subtler offenses as well. For example, the stealing of goods or honest services dampens our enthusiasm to believe in one another, to count on honesty, and to practice charity. An "If I need it—I'll take it" attitude causes ordinary citizens to bolt their doors and secure their cars.

These kinds of injustices also exist in the business world. Greedy bosses rob low-income wage earners of their hope for a better life. Liars steal another's reputation or their hard-earned position.[1]

Say that one's customarily high level of performance slips because of circumstances beyond one's control. Suddenly one hears "over the grapevine" that he or she is unreliable.

Now, instead of attending to the work at hand, this unfairly maligned employee has to engage in "damage control." The stealing of another person's honor by gossip or by the purposeful misinterpretation of his or her intentions is a violation of this commandment, too. Such thievery of the heart hurts. It deforms one's character in the eyes of others.

The promise inherent in the seventh commandment is that we must be willing to make restitution for stealing another's material or spiritual property. It is our responsibility to do so either by returning the goods we have taken or by restoring the trust we have broken.

Disobeying this commandment hampers the quest for peace and joy individually as well as between people. It causes the breakdown of these and many other virtues in society.

RESTORING HUMAN DIGNITY

The collapse of human values typically takes its toll on those least able to defend themselves. Think of how often the elderly are victimized not only by thieves but also by the demeaning aftereffects of stealing.

"I remember the time when we left our doors open all summer," an elderly neighbor once told us, "but that's a thing of the past. They'll steal you blind if they could." We would have liked to rejuvenate in this gentleman the gift of trust in the innate goodness of the human spirit, but he had been robbed twice. Now he lives in fear and eyes strangers suspiciously. Did the thieves know or care when they stole from his house that they also robbed in great part his reason for living in peace and joy?

Blatant robbery takes its toll, but emotional neglect can

be as treacherous to character formation. Whether we intend to do so or not, we can rob people of their dignity with devastating results. It is our responsibility before God to try to make at least partial restitution, certainly for our own offenses but even for those inflicted by other people. This fact was brought home to us on one memorable occasion. We went to investigate a nursing home to accommodate the needs of Susan's mother whose Alzheimer's disease had taken a turn for the worse.

We were standing in the hallway, waiting for an appointment with the administrative staff, when we glanced up and saw a petite, pleasant looking lady with bobbed grey hair shuffling toward us. She was wearing dark sunglasses.

When she got nearer to us, we smiled, greeted her warmly, and asked, "How are you today?"

She paused for a moment and replied, "I'm nothing."

Her answer startled us so much that we blurted out almost in one voice, "What do you mean you're nothing? You're somebody to us!"

She started to walk away, then paused when Susan called after her: "Do you know why we think you're somebody? You look like a woman we know and love. (We were thinking, of course, of Susan's own mother.) We bet you like to cook like she does."

"Maybe," the woman replied.

Encouraged by her hesitant response, Susan continued, "In fact, you look Polish. Are you Polish?"

She straightened up smartly and replied, "Not Polish, Lithuanian. That's what I am."

"What do you like to cook?" She named a favorite Lithuanian dish. "How do you make it?" Suddenly, as if we had tapped into the hiding place of a long buried treasure, this old "nothing" recited in perfect order the ingredients for the preparation of her recipe for Easter bread. It was an excellent rendering. She also recited the baking process from start to finish out of lived experience, not from a cookbook.

We listened intently and then Susan said, "That's marvelous! We can imagine people from all over the neighborhood wanting a taste of your bread. We'll try to remember your recipe. It's terrific. Thanks!"

It was as if we had come to a moment of restitution, as if we were giving her back to herself. "You see what we mean? You really are something, dear lady. You are a bread maker, and bread is the staff of life." She smiled shyly and went on her way. Yet who could forget her?

Isn't it interesting that people who would never think of stealing anything may, through simple neglect, rob those entrusted to their care of the felt sense of their deep worth in God's eyes and of their basic human dignity? While our kind words may have relieved this woman's loneliness and visible depression temporarily, they could not mend the years of neglect that made her think of herself as a "nothing." This episode called our attention to the responsibility we have not only to avoid any form of dishonesty, but also to make restitution for the sufferings people undergo when they feel stripped of their value. What could be worse than robbing people—when they are most vulnerable—of what they most treasure?

How edifying in this regard is the wonderful work of Mother Teresa of Calcutta! Every day she picks up the discards of society, people from whom every shred of human dignity has been stolen by poverty, by a caste system, by disease. She brings these dregs of humanity to her house of the dying and makes restitution for a lifetime of injustice by bathing their bodies, spoon-feeding them warm broth, readying them for their final parting. Despite what has been stolen from them previously, they are now given a great treasure: the silent, tender love of Christ, which is for them of more worth than gold.

What is worse? Stealing a person's purse or robbing that person of his or her identity? While financial restitution may not be possible, spiritual restoration of stolen goods is. If we have lost the art of keeping that spark of dignity alive in people, if we have grown callous to their need for loving treatment, then we are at risk of robbing them not only of their reason for living, but of their right to life. Some toss it away like so much debris.

Is there not an indelible link between killing and stealing? These are the two gravest problems we face in a predominantly functional culture. It is as if the Lord is saying to us, *"You must not do these hurtful things to one another because all of you will ultimately pay the price."* That is why we must try to understand this commandment, not only in materialistic but also in spiritual terms.

A SPIRITUAL TREASURE WE MUST NOT STEAL

People are of immense value in the eternal treasury of God's love. Money cannot match our worth in his eyes. Even in the darkest hour, we are embraced by the luminosity of unending love. God's care for us is everlasting. It is as if humankind, despite sin, has stolen his heart. He has given each of us a unique communal life call. We are invited to be of service to the society in which we are placed by Divine Providence. We are free to choose between good and evil, however many pressures may be upon us.

Our character is incarnated. This means we are an intertwining unity of body, mind, and spirit. To survive, we need the basics of food, clothing, and shelter. These make human life bearable. We have no right to snatch them away at the expense of others. In economically deprived countries, whole groups of people, such as migrant workers, become the victims of greedy landowners who treat them as expendable commodities. When the things they need for a decent standard of living are taken from them, with no intention of restitution, something dies in their spirit.

Stealing not only deprives persons of their rights as owners, it strips them of their trust. A young woman told us that when her apartment was robbed, even though she was not there, the feeling she had for months thereafter was not only one of loss of several items precious to her, but also a sensation that her very personhood had been pillaged. She said, "It was a little like being raped."

Stealing is a serious violation of our right to life, liberty, and the pursuit of happiness. Even Jesus knew that. Everything he owned was taken from him. He was spat upon, scourged, and crowned with thorns. His accusers cast lots for his garment. Worst of all, the murderous crowd to whom he was released for crucifixion sought to steal the truth of his life. Happily for us the Father had another plan. What could be a more splendid or fitting end to his life than the divine restitution we celebrate as his resurrection?

THREE SINFUL DISORIENTATIONS

The three most sinful disorientations or character deformations with which we humans have to grapple are power, pleasure, and possession. It was with these three temptations that the devil tried to ensnare Jesus in the desert (see Luke 4:1-13). He tempted him with power when he promised to make Jesus a king; with pleasure when he offered Our Lord bread; and with possession when he showed him all the kingdoms of the world that would be his if only he would bow down and worship Satan. Jesus rebuffed each enticement in turn.

The temptation of power. Satan could not deter Jesus from his purpose in life by promising him earthly power and glory. In fact, to resist this violation of the seventh commandment, Jesus reminded his tempter of the first: "You shall worship the Lord, your God, and him alone shall you serve" (Lk 4:8).

As Jesus shows us in his answer to Satan, the power pressure can be counteracted by the first commandment. Since the Lord is God, we are not to place the false gods of status and worldly prestige before him.

The temptation of pleasure. Humanly speaking, Jesus was probably hungry after fasting for so long, but he saw that by taking food from the devil he would not be satisfying a legitimate bodily need but succumbing to the temptation to be robbed of his life's mission. Thus he could thwart the devil's intention by telling him, "One does not live on bread alone" (Lk 4:4). Christ fed himself spiritually on every word of God, and so must we. We can do the same if we keep our eyes focused on a more transcendent goal. Remember also that the pressure to make pleasure our main purpose is definitely counteracted in another context by the sixth commandment, forbidding us to commit adultery.

The temptation to possess. In refusing to worship Satan, Jesus forfeited all false claims to worldly wealth. It is this third temptation that the seventh commandment specifically addresses. Jesus rebuffed the pressure to possess, but if we are not careful, we can easily be possessed by our possessions. Many are caught in the snares set by a materialistic world. All they think about is what they own, how they can hold on to it, how to increase it, and what they have to do to make sure nobody else gets it. The pressure to possess can entrap us before we know it.

A researcher may be so caught up in seeking funding for a pet project that, before he knows it, he begins to steal quality time from his family. Another person may be driven by a "publish or perish" mentality to compromise the integrity of his or her work to achieve public acclaim, fast promotion, or monetary reward. There are innumerable warnings in Holy Scripture about this enslavement to having.

Ownership as such is not the issue. The Bible names many people who possessed wealth (Abraham, for one, Nicodemus, for another), yet whose lives on the whole were pleasing to God. This proves that possession as such is not a sin. What makes it sinful is our inordinate attachment to wealth. It can be so great that we refuse to help the poor. We forfeit the call to be good stewards of what belongs ultimately to God. That is why Jesus said, "No one can serve two masters. He will either hate one and love the other, or be devoted to one and despise the other. You cannot serve God and Mammon" (Mt 7:24).

In telling us not to steal, the Lord helps us to see that nothing is worth more than the salvation of our immortal soul. For "what profit is there for one to gain the whole world yet lose or forfeit himself?" (Lk 9:25).

In summary, we are often lured by powerful temptations to satisfy our voracious appetites to have (power), to devour (pleasure), and to hold (possession). The seventh commandment acts, as do all Ten Commandments, as preventive medicine. If we follow it, we are less likely to be caught in these devilish snares.

BECOMING RESPONSIBLE STEWARDS

All that we possess has been given to us by God. We are stewards, called to oversee and protect God's property. We are not owners. We are to share the gifts God bestows on us with others as well as to make restitution for anything that is stolen.

The seventh commandment, like those that preceded it and those that follow it, aims to reform inclinations in us toward sin in its subtle or overt expressions. Without a personal relationship with the Lord, this kind of reformation is impossible. We cannot live the commandments to the full unless we draw close to Christ. We need to be so conscious of his love, grace, and goodness, of his commitment to save us, that we become disinclined to ever act contrary to his commands.

Obedience to the commandments frees us *from* the weight of sin while freeing us *for* the joys of simple living and the noncompetitive grace of stewardship. Through obedience we come to know Jesus most intimately. This knowledge of the heart marks the start of our transformation: from casual adherence to the veneer of the commandments to profound commitment to their implications for our spiritual maturity.

When Scripture warns against acquiring the wrong kind of riches—those gained by stockpiling wealth and oppressing the poor—it is because our salvation is at stake. When money becomes our "god," there is no room left for a true person-to-Person intimacy with God. We steal the time we ought to spend with him to feed our avaricious needs. No matter how much stuff we acquire, it is never enough.

This commandment drives home the point that to check avarice we must also refuse to steal the time God wants us to spend with him. Here, too, we must be responsible stewards.

Think of Mary and Martha (see Luke 10:38-42). Jesus loved both of his friends, but for this special visit he wanted Martha to be present to him, too. She should not be busy with other things, but pay attention to his offer of intimacy, as Mary did. Mary sat at the feet of Jesus and listened. She contemplated him first, as a good steward would, for only then could she serve him.

We must not rob God of the opportunity to show us that his love is enough for us. If the Lord comes first in our life, if we make his presence our foremost priority, then the peace and joy we receive from him already on earth will be of more worth than anything money can buy. He disentangles us from the snares of materialism and consumerism. He frees us from the danger of being possessed by our possessions. He gives us the ability to distinguish between wants and needs.

To become good stewards and to overcome the obstacles forbidden by the seventh commandment, we must frequently pray:

My Lord and my God, I believe with all my heart that your love is enough for me. You know what I want, and you know what I need. You will show me what is good for me, and you will see to it that I receive it in accordance with your will. What you offer me is deeply satisfying. I can't imagine what I've done to deserve such spiritual treasures! Teach me now to share them generously with others.

If our Lord is not enough, our hunger for other imagined "enoughs" (power, pleasure, possession) ends up being insatiable. Selfishness spreads like a blight in our world. All of us are touched by it in one way or another.

The following words of Martin Luther offer a good summary of what we believe to be at the heart of the seventh commandment's directives for virtuous character building in response to divine grace:

> Here you have a rich Lord *[in contrast to all the ways in which we try to get rich, which end up making us horribly poor from the point of view of spiritual maturity]*. Surely he is sufficient for your needs and will let you lack or want nothing. Thus, with a happy conscience you can enjoy a hundred times more than you could scrape together by perfidy and injustice. Whoever does not desire this blessing *[the blessing of a deeply transformed heart and a profoundly reformed approach to material as well as spiritual things]* will find wrath and misfortune enough.[2]

Let us, therefore, continue to ask for the grace not to be guilty of either stealing the rightful possessions of others, or robbing them of their dignity. Trusting that God knows what we need, even before we ask, let us be good and faithful servants, who witness to God's freely offered generosity in a world prone to put a price tag on everything.

TIME TO REFLECT ON
THE SEVENTH COMMANDMENT

Step Seven: Restitution

This commandment communicates God's idea on how we ought to treat property. Nobody has the right to take what does not belong to him, though we humans do so all the time. While a privileged few seem to have more than the many, there are enough resources on earth to guarantee that no one should ever want for the necessities of life such as food, shelter, and clothing. The basics for survival are God-given gifts, provided we follow the way of compassionate stewardship and do not steal.

The seventh commandment insists that we learn the meaning of responsible ownership and that even the seemingly most innocent and petty cases of stealing violate that right. We can own things on the condition that we use them responsibly. Lest greed get the best of us, we should keep in mind the privileges and obligations ownership brings. The property God entrusts to us must in some way foster the good of all.

In the end we are owners of nothing; we are only borrowers living for a while in God's world. To think it belongs ultimately to us is but an illusion. We are stewards of his creation. Thus we must be givers, not takers, for, as the Book of Proverbs teaches (19:17): "He who has compassion on the poor lends to the Lord, and he will repay him for his good deed."[3]

QUESTIONS FOR REFLECTION

1. Do I secretly condone the story of Robin Hood and his merry band, thinking it is acceptable to rob from the rich to give to the poor, or that the poor are justified for violating this commandment? What can I do to counter the widespread stealing and wanton destruction of property that downgrades our society?

Your Thoughts:

2. Does the threat of theft make me suspicious of all strangers? Am I overly protective of my possessions? At some time in my life have I been guilty of stealing something? Do I feel remorse? Did I try to make restitution?

Your Thoughts:

3. In the light of the seventh commandment, how can I moderate my inordinate attachment to the goods of this world and relearn to value the simplification of life? What will it take to make me imitate the generosity of the Lord, who although he was rich, yet for our sake became poor "so that by his poverty, [we] might become rich" (2 Cor 8:9)?

Your Thoughts:

Stewardship of Your Creation

Let us celebrate
Epiphanies that penetrate
Peace-filled people,
Highlighting your abiding
In suffering humanity.
Keep us from feeling low
If others belittle in us
What you bestow.

Grant us gratefulness for your gifts,
Deepening our ability for stewardship
Of your creation.
Let us not feel less,
Teach us to redress
Pain inflicted
On your stewards, Lord.

If we meet little ones
Oppressed and burdened by defeat,
Let us instill
Strength of will
In those that are lame,
Slain by indignity and shame
Heaped upon them by the slick and arrogant.

May we redress unfairness
By kindling again
The dying ember of dignity divine
Squelched in the poor by callous degradation.

And every day, unceasingly pray
For those caught on the greedy way
Of power and possession,
Their mind and heart a restless mill
Driven by the anxious will
To gain more and more,
Seduced by the idle lore
That much rather than less
Means always happiness.

Stealing, killing, lying,
A culture dying
In the grip of greed
Let us pluck the poisonous weed.
That blurs the border between good and bad,
Smothering dreams with wet blankets of thievery,
And eating away heart's purity.

—Fr. Adrian van Kaam

E I G H T

THE EIGHTH COMMANDMENT:

*"You Shall Not Bear
False Witness against
Your Neighbor."*

The Way of Reconciliation

If, then, you heed all that I command you, follow my ways, and please me by keeping my statutes and my commandments like my servant David, I will be with you. I will establish for you, as I did for David, a lasting dynasty; I will give Israel to you.

1 Kings 11:38

Stealing, understood materially or spiritually, requires restitution. False witness distorts the truth and diminishes trust. Deceiving others makes a new demand on us: It calls for a restoration of truthful relations with ourselves, others, and God. In short, the demand in this commandment is for reconciliation. God has to know that we are sorry for not telling the truth. Others need to sense that we regret hurting them in this way. And we have to prove to ourselves and them that we are not habitual liars.

Lying nips away at emergent virtue like a caterpillar devours bit by bit each leaf on a branch until all the green is gone. The process seems to take a long time, but before we know it, the tree is bare. The line between truth and falsehood shrinks and with it goes the possibility for peace and joy in our hearts and in formerly trusting relationships.

To obey this commandment requires not only a radical

return to telling the truth (while knowing discreetly when and to whom and if we ought to "tell all"); it also requires examining why lying is so reprehensible in God's eyes. Maybe it's because this sin, more than any other, severed the original covenant between us and our Creator.

DEFORMATIVE CONSEQUENCES OF LYING

The fall of humankind began with a lie. The serpent lied to Eve, and she believed him. She recounted the evil tale to Adam, and he believed her. The consequences of their distortion of truth as well as their self-deception were immediate and devastating. Both were banished from the Garden of Eden, where humans once strolled hand-in-hand with God. From that point in time to this, lying has fractured trust and love. It deforms our character, clouding the truth of who we are and who God is.

Many forces paralyze our capacity to listen to what God is asking of us: pride, self-deception, seductive ploys to confuse others, so as to take advantage of their gullibility or to look smooth in their eyes. We can lie our way through life, but the sad news is that we may be the first to falter. "A lie has short legs." This frequently quoted childhood saying is a good reminder that bearing false witness backfires on us. We go astray. We drift away lie by lie from the loving Being who is at the center of our life.

If we violate the integrity of our speech, we pay the price. Corruption becomes a casual affair: people break promises using elaborate cover-ups or "little white lies;" everyone blaming everyone else for his or her mistakes. Before long, detours and misdirections become so customary that we lose our course. When this happens, we hate to admit it. We are lost in a maze of lies while we resist the call to reconciliation.

Jesus himself was the victim of people's radical disobedience of this commandment. The lies they told about him eventually took his life, but no amount of false witness could smother the truth of his words. Even on the cross, he asked the Father to forgive those liars who did not know what they were doing (see Luke 22:34).

The wider the ditch of lies we dig between us and God, the deeper must be the reconciliation. Only then can the character deformation caused by falsehood begin to diminish.

Consider Peter, Jesus' true friend. When the hour came to support the Master, what did Peter do? He lied—he denied that he knew Jesus. Unlike Judas, who betrayed him, seemingly without remorse, Peter must have sensed that his life would come to nothing unless the Master forgave him. After denying Jesus three times, he wept bitterly (see Mark 14:66-72). The scene of their reconciliation, when they shared a meal by the sea and reconfirmed their love for one another, is among the most touching in Scripture. There Jesus asks Peter to declare his love three times; then he commissions him to feed his lambs and tend his sheep, in effect, to nourish them with the truth of his words, even if doing so will in due time cost Peter his life, too (see John 21:15-19).

FINDING OUR WAY BACK
TO THE LIGHT OF TRUTH

Though character formation has to wade through the fog of original sin, God remains the God of our heart. He asks us continually: *Why do you persist in lying to yourselves and others when my truth sets you free?*

God calls us to leave the dark corridors of deception and return to the full light of day. Our condition is such that its transformation in Christ requires many "thou shalt nots." Progress to peace and joy is hampered by falsehood, but not hopelessly. The sticky webs of ignorance of our true transcendent call entrap us, but they need not destroy us if the commandments become our rule of life. They communicate to every person, even the greatest liars and sinners, that reconciliation with God, that restarting our life on the firm footage of his truth, is always possible. This revelation is our way into the light.

Of what use is it to lie to ourselves when we know how fallible we are? Of what use is it to lie to others when by our false witness we end up condemning ourselves? The Apostle James explains that the tongue is a small member and yet it has great pretensions. He says:

> Consider how a small fire can set a huge forest ablaze. The tongue is also a fire. It exists among our members as a world of malice, defiling the whole body and setting the entire course of our lives on fire...   **James 3:5-6**

If we lie about people out of envy or jealousy, fabricating stories to make them look bad, it is like striking a match in a parched forest. Little twigs and large timbers equally catch fire.

Lies are mean-spirited. They spread like smoky cinders in the wind. People who thrive on falsehood fan the fires with their own exaggerations. Soon an "innocent" lie here, a "small fib" there, may become an inferno.

A priest was talking to a woman who lied habitually about her neighbor. "For your penance," he said, "take a bag of feathers and climb up to your attic, open the window and throw them out. Then go down into the yard and pick each of them up. That will give you some idea of how your lies scatter the truth and how difficult it is to regain your own integrity and be reconciled with your neighbor." Whether this story is true or not, it's a good illustration of how character distortion results when we disobey this commandment.

We must find our way back to the light of truth. The Apostle Paul says in his Letter to the Ephesians: "Therefore, putting away falsehood, speak the truth, each one to his neighbor, for we are members one of another" (Eph 4:25). Paul's words are evocative. If we are members of one Body, then to bear false witness against a sister or brother is a despicable thing to do. Victims of our lying tongue are left defenseless. When we vilify them in private or in public, when we gossip about them, we are not only hurting them—we are also hurting ourselves.

Lying chips away at the mosaic of truth crafted by God in all Ten Commandments. The attainment of peace and joy is impossible if we do not reconcile ourselves to his way of graced formation, reformation, and transformation.

Walking in the truth is not a matter of telling everything to everybody one knows. Moral reservation or discretion is acceptable, as when negotiators are trying to reconcile warring factions. Falsehood must be peeled away slowly from the truth, like layers of an onion, to reveal its core. In addition to discretion, the virtue of discernment is also needed. Diplomats have to sift through layers of mutually destructive untruths to find some common ground of agreement.

This commandment does not imply that the disclosure of

every private detail of our life is necessary or advisable. It also covers issues of confidentiality. When and to whom can we talk without jeopardizing another's integrity, or in any way harming another's reputation?

There is a time and a place for sharing and for withholding. In the words of the Eastern spiritual master St. Isaac of Nineveh, "If you love truth, be a lover of silence."[1] The spiritual masters especially commend silence when it comes to relating our religious experiences. These are easily distorted or exaggerated by false witness. We ought to follow the advice first penned by the psalmist: "Desist! and confess that I am God..." (Ps 46:11).

What ought to be kept secret and what ought to be told is a judgment call each person has to make. We witness to our beliefs one way at a party, another at a funeral. We always have to take the situation into account without making it the only determining factor. Telling the truth indiscriminantly can lead our listeners to disbelieve us or to think that we are exaggerating. To them we may sound like the little boy who cried "Wolf!" once too often.

Undoubtedly, character maturation has to do with mastering the art of knowing what we ought and ought not to divulge about ourselves or others. What "witnessing" causes unnecessary trouble? What is absolutely necessary, courageous, and prophetic? People who use the media as newscasters or writers especially need to develop a strong moral conscience. They are in a privileged place to deceive or to tell the truth in a way that demeans or serves a free society.[2]

Living in a truthful way, resistant to falsehood, means celebrating the good wherever we find it. Some people have a knack for dressing nicely; others write beautiful poetry or have the reputation of being pleasantly entertaining. Let the truth of their being shine forth. Bear loving witness to it. Do not label anyone as less. Never falsify their unique contribution.

MOVING FROM FALSE WITNESS TO TRUE RECONCILIATION

This step to peace and joy, like the others we have climbed thus far, presupposes that people are good at heart and that God believes that we are capable of such obedience. The commandments offer us the route from false witness to reconciliation with our Creator. Whatever limits we have are forgivable in his eyes as long as we acknowledge our faults and try to do better.

This eighth commandment makes no bones about what we must do. As disciples of Christ, we are to live in the truth (see 1 John 1:6). It warns us of the grave consequences of living in the darkness of deception and of the havoc it can create between us and our neighbor. Nothing, *The Catechism* says, so radically erodes trust, nothing makes such a mockery out of Christ's unconditional love for us, than refusing to commit ourselves to "moral uprightness" [2464].

False witness undermines the foundations of the covenant made by God, the source of all truth, with his Chosen People. It clouds our conscience (see Acts 24:16) and "tears apart the fabric of social relationships" [2486].[3]

The teller of truth and the teller of lies cannot live at ease with one another unless the liar reforms his or her ways. Deception exacts a price, whether people willfully falsify the truth or lie indirectly.

Unmasking deception is a long process. People who habitually exaggerate the truth to be impressive often create a climate of suspicion. They have a way of drawing others into a murky fog of prefabrication. But those who tell "fish stories" may find it difficult to unlearn this custom. Character building depends on the reformation of such bad habits.

How should we protect ourselves from the influence of people who seem unable to discern fact from fiction? A good question. At times we may be obliged to expose their lies. At other times, feeling ourselves alone and defenseless, we may have to avoid liars or commend them to God for his protection!

The climate of confusion that lying produces is fertile ground for the devil, who "roams around seeking whom he may devour" (1 Pt 5:8). In the end, we must turn to Jesus, who calls us to live in the Spirit, and who will lead us into the light of truth (see John 16:13). Then this unconditional love of the truth will become second nature to us, for our *yes* will mean *yes*, and our *no* will mean *no* (see Matthew 5:37).

Addressing the formative implications of this commandment, the reformer Martin Luther wrote a fitting summary of our concerns:

No one shall harm his neighbor whether friend or foe, with his tongue. No one shall speak evil of him whether truly or falsely unless it is done with proper authority for his improvement. A person should use his tongue to speak only good of everyone, to cover his neighbor's sins and infirmities, to overlook them and to clothe and fill them with his own honor. Our chief reason for doing so should be the one which Christ indicates in the Gospel and which he means to embrace all the commandments concerning our neighbor. Whatever you wish for [others] to do to you, do so to them.[4]

TIME TO REFLECT ON
THE EIGHTH COMMANDMENT

Step Eight: Reconciliation

This commandment prohibits falsifying reality. It promises that by not deceiving ourselves or distorting the truth to implicate others, we shall solidify our virtuous character and find renewed peace and joy.

God wills the truth, God tells the truth, and so should we. It is morally reprehensible to lie under oath, but it is equally wrong to lie as a matter of course, not out of self-protection or self-defense but simply because we have forgotten how to tell the truth.

In the Old Testament there is no ambiguity about this commandment: God's word is true because he is the source of all truth. It is by his law of truth that we are to live. Thus we read in Psalms 119:30-32:

The way of truth I have chosen;
I have set your ordinances before me.
I cling to your decrees; O Lord,
let me not be put to shame.
I will run the way of your commands,
when you give me a docile heart.

It is in our Lord Jesus Christ that the whole truth of God's way has been revealed to us. He is the light of the world, full of grace and truth (see John 1:14; 8:12; 14:6). Believing in him lifts the veil of darkness covering our eyes because of sin (see John 12:46). In Matthew's Gospel, Jesus teaches us the way of truth with characteristic clarity:

Again you have heard that it was said to your ancestors, "Do not take a false oath, but make good to the Lord all that you vow." But I say to you, do not swear at all; not by heaven, for it is God's throne; nor by the earth, for it is his footstool; nor by Jerusalem, for it is the city of the great King. Do not swear by your head, for you cannot make a single hair white or black. Let your "Yes" mean "Yes," and your "No" mean "No." Anything more is from the evil one. **Matthew 5:33-37**

The eighth commandment prohibits the distortion or misrepresentation of the truth in our dealings with family members, friends, neighbors, coworkers, and others who expect us to say what we mean and mean what we say. The purpose of this divine directive is to help us to experience the truth that sets us free (see John 8:32; 17:17).

QUESTIONS FOR REFLECTION

1. In a world where everything from "little white lies" to perjury seems a matter of course, what happens when I do not stand behind the truth of my words? If candor with self, others, and God is as necessary a disposition as discretion, why doesn't adherence to the truth direct all my exchanges?

Your Thoughts:

2. Am I willing to pay the price of lying, malicious gossip, and giving false reports? Does it not hurt me and everyone when corruption becomes a casual affair? When people break more promises than they keep? When trust in a shared task falls to pieces? How can I reverse this erosion of mutual confidence and operate with a clear conscience? What ought I to express in this situation? What ought to be withheld for the time being, and from whom?

Your Thoughts:

3. If truth is to be cultivated in my life like a good fruit-bearing tree, how can I refrain from ever diminishing the reputation of another person by rash judgment, detraction, calumny, or the kind of flattery or adulation that confirms a malicious act? Do I ever brag about offenses against the truth or lying with an intention to deceive or to lead another person into error? Have I deliberately given false witness or been guilty of perjury? What prevents me from taking to heart the injunction of the Apostle Paul: "You should put away the old self of your former way of life, corrupted through deceitful desires, and be renewed in the spirit of your minds, and put on the new self, created in God's way in righteousness and holiness of truth" (Eph 4:22-24)?

Your Thoughts:

Reconciling Word and Deed

Reconciliation, beacon bright
On my journey in the night,
Wayside sign to my destiny in time,
Deepen my fidelity to unfolding harmony,
Rising beyond blind boundaries of dissonance,
In a dance of reconciling word and deed.

Reconciliation, help us to meet on
   common ground,
No longer bound to the paralyzing plight
Of prejudice and pride
That steals our peace.

Reconciliation, let us deal with people
In respect for each one's dignity,
Granted by the Mystery.
Let us not lie, but believe
In the better side of those
Who bring us grief.

Reconciliation, open us to the deepest "why"
Escaping our myopic eye.
Are people lying due to lack of love?
Can they not get along because some,
Forgetful of their dignity,
Betray their fidelity?
Do they speak their won'ts
To release a secret stress,
Leaving them less able to bear with life?
Are they crippled by the strife

To survive obstacles that, like barnacles,
Slow down their leaking ship
In clouds of mist and foam?
Why are they so alone,
Dwellers without a home,
Travelers in desert lands
Roamed by hostile bands,
Endless west of the unknown?

The song of reconciliation
Sings in our tired life, melting the strife,
Paving a smoother way for those who went astray.
In reconciliation, with wise discretion,
Let us bend toward those sent
On a journey strange to our taste.
What seems to be a waste
May lead them to a place
Of peace and grace,
A new springtime of the Divine.

—Fr. Adrian van Kaam

N I N E

THE NINTH COMMANDMENT:

*"You Shall Not Covet
Your Neighbor's Wife."*

The Way of Admiration

*He who keeps the commandment experiences no evil,
and the wise man's heart knows times and judg-
ments, for there is a time and a judgment for everything. Yet it is a great affliction for man that he is
ignorant of what is to come; for who will make
known to him how it will be?* **Ecclesiastes 8:5-7**

The last two commandments of the Decalogue target the
same obstacle to finding lasting peace and joy in this life:
covetousness. Classical spiritual masters like St. Anthony of
Egypt, St. Catherine of Siena, and St. John of the Cross, to
name only a few, would see covetousness as inordinate
attachment, or clinging to what is less as if it were God. To
covet that which is less than God in the first place is to forfeit
our ability to admire people and things from a respectable
distance. We want to put them in our orbit or to possess
them with no sense of their rightful owner, who, in the last
analysis, is not us but the Divine Giver of all goods.

Covetousness merits two commandments because in
some way it violates the other eight by fostering idolatry, disrespect, desecration, disobedience, even murder or crimes of
passion, adultery, robbery, and deceit. The ninth and tenth
commandments rivet our attention once more on the basic
elements of formation for a happy life and a healthy soul
found in all Ten Commandments. If we do not love God
above anyone or anything else, if we do not care for our

neighbors as we take care of ourselves, covetousness is the result. It cancels peace and joy in our own and others' lives.

The covetous eye knows nothing of admiration or consideration. The dispositions it forms within us are deeply deformative, poisoning our whole spirit. Where covetousness reigns, other evils are sure to be found. Envy displaces admiration, strife disrupts neighborly peace, hatred shatters joy. When David coveted Bathsheba, the wife of Uriah, God was greatly displeased, for David plotted to kill Bathsheba's husband so he could marry her (see 2 Samuel 11:27). Though God loved David the sinner, he abhorred his sin. Whenever covetousness supersedes detached admiration, a wrong is done.

None of us, whether married or single, clerical or lay, can exonerate ourselves from this commandment. We must take a careful look at our lives. In other words, do we reverence our relationships as gifts of God? Do we avoid placing ourselves in compromising situations that erode the respectful distance necessary for proper detachment from what is not ours? Have we committed ourselves to obeying God's commands to such a degree that our willful desires are increasingly subjected to the light of the Spirit?

CHARACTER REFORMATION
THROUGH ADMIRATION

Reforming a covetous heart is a painful process. Like any purgation it takes time. It may mean, on the one hand, intensifying our love for God by detaching ourselves from lesser loves that bind us to what is not ours in the first place. On the other hand, it does mean fastening our hearts so much on God that we begin to look toward him all the time in contemplative admiration. We love God for his own sake and covet no other person as a source of ultimate satisfaction. This commandment forbids inordinate attachment to lesser affections—not by destroying them, but by absorbing them into the love of God.

The more God sees us loving him with purity of heart and charity (not covetousness) toward our neighbor, the more we are caught up in admiration of the Divine. God, not another person's spouse, takes our breath away!

Here prohibition ceases and promise increases. We dwell on God in loving adoration, in contemplative admiration. As a result, we gravitate toward people whose goodness confirms our faith, heightens our hope, and deepens our love for God and neighbor. In them we catch a glimpse of the face of Christ behind all faces.

Jesus blesses those who turn from covetousness to admiration. They embody the Christ-like dispositions enumerated by the Apostle Paul in his Epistle to the Galatians (5:22-23): "love, joy, peace, patience, kindness, generosity, faithfulness, gentleness, and self-control." No longer yielding to self-indulgence, they imitate the Lord Jesus Christ. They live the commandments instead of only memorizing them.

Indecency, seduction, manipulation—such forms of impurity fade into the night of spiritual cleansing. The effects of this reformation are seen, as Paul says in his Letter to the Ephesians, "in every kind of goodness and righteousness and truth" (Eph 5:9). The love of God enables the friends of God to cease coveting what does not belong to them or what does not lead them to him. His grace has so purified their hearts that they have no other aim than to do what God wills and commands.

SOURCES OF COVETOUS
CHARACTER DEFORMATION

Lurking behind any and all forms of covetous behavior is the egoism that seeks its own self-aggrandizing gratification, often at the expense of others and in violation of God's specific commands. Countering this devastating divisiveness is the intention to craft an undivided heart, in short, to seek the glory of God and the good of others.

A major obstacle to purity of heart is any form of what St. John of the Cross calls "spiritual lust."[1] What concerns him are not only obvious sins against purity (like coveting another's spouse), but any feelings or attachments that interfere with our first commitment to love God with our whole being and others as ourselves. It is wise to acknowledge such feelings when they flare up because in themselves they are not sinful. What counts is redirecting our attention to God and following the leading of his Spirit.

That is the reason spiritual masters insist on the importance of modesty and custody of the eyes. We must guard our heart lest we lose ourselves in the endless wanderings or covetous glances oblivious to the stirrings of grace. The Eastern church fathers, like St. Macarius, tell us that grace passes by way of the heart into the whole of our nature. What if we are so busy looking outward that we fail to attend to the inward directions, beckoning our attention and will to turn to God?

Living in contemplative admiration dampens the fires of covetous envy. Admiration is a mode of blessedness more than of accomplishment. It is abiding in stillness more than in restlessness or agitation. Admiration is a mode of being *in* the world more than *at* the world. It is a stirring of the heart, transformed by means of wonder more than by modes of mastery.

Admiration enables us to wait upon the revelation of God's nearness in everyday encounters with our neighbors without any sense of haste or coercion. An epiphany of the Most High may happen when we least expect it. We now know how to treat it delicately. We do not pounce upon grace like greedy greyhounds, as the author of *The Cloud of Unknowing* says.[2] Rather we wait admiringly upon the mystery in the midst of everydayness. We take the risk of abandoning the false sense of security that comes when we are in charge. We release our covetous grip on life and give ourselves over to God, glorifying him with one heart and voice.

FROM COVETOUSNESS TO
CONVERSION OF HEART

In his book *Crossing the Threshold of Hope*, Pope John Paul II explains what it means to accept the moral demands God places on us, and at the same time to admire the saving love, the lasting hope, the true beauty such obedience brings.

God's demands never exceed our ability to obey, nor does God ask us to conform to his will without the gift of his grace. *"To accept the Gospel's demands,"* says the Pope, *"means to affirm all of our humanity, to see in it the beauty desired by God."*[3] He then demonstrates that acceptance of the commandments increases peace and joy:

The world is full of proof of the saving and redemptive power that the Gospels proclaim with even greater frequency than they recall demands of the moral life. How many people there are in the world whose daily lives attest to the possibility of living out the morality of the Gospel! Experience shows that a successful human life cannot be other than a life like theirs.[4]

What we admire in such people is their core form or "heart." We see in them a noble character, so inwardly fixed on God that nothing else belonging to a neighbor can grab their attention, grip their imagination, or grate on their memory. Their heart is where it should be: It is with God. Through God they are able to admire every good and perfect gift (see James 1:17).

Martin Luther explains in his meditation on the ninth commandment why conversion of heart is necessary to dilute the strength of covetous desires:

We are commanded not to desire harm to our neighbor, nor become accessory to it, nor give occasion for it; we are willingly to leave him what is his, and promote and protect whatever may be profitable and serviceable to him, as we wish that he would do to us. Thus these commandments are directed especially against envy and miserable covetousness, God's purpose being to destroy all the roots and causes of our injuries to our neighbors. Therefore he sets it forth in plain words: "You shall not covet," etc. Above all, he wants our hearts to be pure, even though as long as we live here we cannot reach that ideal. So this commandment accuses us and shows just how upright we really are in God's sight.[5]

Luther, like his much admired mentor St. Augustine, realizes that conversion of heart is a lifelong process. It should not surprise us that St. Augustine saw envy as "*the* diabolical sin." From it, St. Gregory the Great, as cited in *The Catechism*, said, "are born hatred, detraction, calumny, joy caused by the misfortune of a neighbor, and displeasure caused by [another's] prosperity" [2539].

Envy eats away like a slow-acting poison at our heart. We cannot easily turn away from its destructive force unless we turn in awe and admiration toward the goodness of creation and the God who has made all that the eye can see or the ear can hear. Why envy anyone? Submit this unruly passion to the cooling breeze of reason and the quiet splendor of a higher love-will for God, for God alone can satisfy our heart's desires.

A word that has almost been cast out of our vocabulary makes the prohibition side of this commandment a step toward its promise of conversion of heart and purification of vision. This word offers a corrective to the social climate in which we live today where permissiveness and moral decay prevail. The word we mean is "modesty." Its implications for character formation have been summarized beautifully in *The Catechism:*

Purity requires *modesty*, an integral part of temperance. Modesty protects the intimate center of the person. It means refusing to unveil what should remain hidden. It is ordered to chastity to whose sensitivity it bears witness. It guides how one looks at others and behaves toward them in conformity with the dignity of persons and their solidarity.

Modesty protects the mystery of persons and their love. It encourages patience and moderation in loving relationships; it requires that the conditions for the definitive giving and commitment of man and woman to one another be fulfilled. Modesty is decency. It inspires one's choice of clothing. It keeps silence or reserve where there is evident risk of unhealthy curiosity. It is discreet.

... [Modesty] protests, for example, against the voyeuristic explorations of the human body in certain advertisements.... [It also] inspires a way of life which makes it possible to resist the allurements of fashion and the pressures of prevailing ideologies [2521-2523].

In short, though the rules of modesty vary from culture to culture wherever it exists, it promotes a mutual respect for human dignity. When modesty drops its guard, so do the inner inhibitions that uphold this commandment. When modesty prevails over lust and envy, its fruits enhance the whole of society. It represents a significant step to the fullness of peace and joy bestowed on us by God's grace.

TIME TO REFLECT ON
THE NINTH COMMANDMENT

Step Nine: Admiration

This commandment offers as a condition for guarding our heart one of the oldest rules of spiritual formation: vigilance. It was practiced by the desert monks of old, and it must be practiced by us in the desert of the modern world, wasted away as it is by the twists and turns of unbounded lust. The things that pleasure us, in violation of the commandments, do not make us happy. Only following God's way can lead us to health of body, mind, and soul.

This way is paved with the solid cement of charity in all things. It is lined with the sturdy trees of chastity. It echoes the universal call to holiness, for Jesus promises us in the Sermon on the Mount that the pure of heart will see God (see Matthew 5:8). To see other people as our neighbors is to see them as temples of the Holy Spirit, as epiphanies of divine beauty, not as objects of lustful envy.

QUESTIONS FOR REFLECTION

1. Why am I so prone to be envious of the people around
me? What prevents me from willing the good where others
are concerned? Why does envy eat away like a slow-acting
poison at my heart? What in me makes me want to snatch
from others what is rightfully theirs?

Your Thoughts:

2. When do I sense, in the words of St. Paul, that my "flesh"
is at war with my "spirit" (see Galatians 5:16-17, 24;
Ephesians 2:3)? Am I aware that looking with lust and
envy at another human being paves the way for more serious sin? Am I ready to submit my unruly passions to the
cooling breeze of reason, to the quiet splendor of a higher
love-will for God, who alone can satisfy my heart's desires?

Your Thoughts:

3. If "out of the heart come evil thoughts, murder, adultery, fornication" (Mt 15:19), how can I concretely practice two of the best, time-tested rules of spiritual formation, namely, vigilance of the heart and modesty of the eyes? How can I learn to live in purity of heart so that I habitually see others and things in God's benevolent light?

Your Thoughts:

Loving Admiration

When earthly hope grows dim
Faith draws us to the rim
Of loving admiration
Silencing the temptation
To refuse the "yes" the soul
Whispers as its inmost goal.
The heart grows tender,
Risks surrender to the epiphany
Of universe and history.
Our "yes" should soar aloft
Like a cable car streaks
Between sunlit snowy peaks
Beyond the valley down below,
The black ravine of gloomy no
That sparks despair, decay
As worms in apples
Spoiled and stale.

Don't look at life with envious eyes,
Don't see it as ill-disposed,
As tight and closed
Within the gilded cage
Of dull tranquility,
Like a bird that lost its melody
And flaps its tired wing
Against the silken bars
But can no longer sing.

The flight of grace
Revives the song of praise
That died on our lips.
Covetous envy gives way
To silent admiration,
Inviting us to acquiesce
In a "yes" of gratefulness,
Admiring family and friends,
Meals, success, a lovely dress,
And every little thing we see and sense,
There is no end to gratefulness,
To always saying "yes,"
Not coveting secretly
What seems to make us less.

You bestowed dignity abundantly
On every human life.
Each one is a sanctuary
Hiding the mystery
Of a mission outshining
In the eyes of angels.

A retarded child,
A sick old woman,
Outcasts of society,
Foreigners talking haltingly,
Each one splendid
As a lustrous opal,
Precious as gold
In the sight of God.

—Fr. Adrian van Kaam

T E N

The Tenth Commandment:

"You Shall Not Covet Your Neighbor's Goods."

The Way of Concelebration

The commandments, "You shall not commit adultery; you shall not kill; you shall not steal; you shall not covet," and whatever other commandment there may be, are summed up in this saying [namely] "You shall love your neighbor as yourself."

Romans 13:9

The tenth commandment shields us from the treacherous winds of jealousy blowing wildly within us because others seem to be more important than we are, or to possess more than we own. Covetousness inclines us to analyze, like stingy clerks counting beans in a produce bin, what others have that we do not. We want to be sure that no one looks better than we do or amasses more than we have. The tenth commandment is thus related to the seventh. Not obeying it may tempt us to steal another's goods.

This covetous deformation of character is a byproduct of pure greed. We find it impossible to be grateful for the gifts others have been given. We are not happy for them. We are jealous and full of ill will.

Maybe we think we can exonerate ourselves from this commandment because we really don't want any more than we have now. But the forms in which covetousness can tighten our hearts are subtle. The tenth commandment teaches us to be wary of them. Maybe we do not covet the new car our neighbor owns because we appear to be perfectly happy with our old beat-up model. But if the truth were known, we ask ourselves every time we look in their driveway, "Who do they think they are, anyway?"

Jealousy is hard to hold in check. It flares up at the least provocation. Overcoming this kind of covetousness, and the greed and ill will it spawns between family members and co-workers, calls for strict vigilance of heart. We need to recognize the first twinges of covetousness when they occur—or it will gain the upper hand.

The best antidote to this aberration is concelebration. It is the disposition of heart that encourages us to celebrate together our personal and communal goods. Instead of focusing on what is missing, we count our blessings.

OBSTACLES BLOCKING CONCELEBRATION

Possessiveness is like a security blanket: We hate to give it up. In a capitalistic society, people are trained early in life to get more and give less. Consumerism and materialism become marks of progress and success, so much so that the disadvantaged are either forgotten or inclined to see themselves only as "have nots." In the latter case, if self-pity for "poor me" predominates, people may covet every good thing others have and live in constant resentment, thus killing their own initiative and creativity. When this happens, the doors to serving others close. Neighborly love dies on the vine. The sparks of avarice keep the furnace of covetousness burning at full power.

This commandment issues a warning: If we do not co-operate with the grace God has given us by being gracious to others, greed will gnaw away at charity's heels like a mean, hungry dog that first chews, then buries a bone. There will be no meat of compassion left to feed the hungry and shelter the poor.

Our consumer society is not much help in this regard. The world of advertising, pop culture, buying and selling blurs the distinction between wants and needs. It teaches us from the time we are young to satisfy our wants whether or not we need a particular item.

A man may have a perfectly good lawn mower, but when his neighbor gets a newer model he wants one, too. This acquisition-at-any-cost approach is self-perpetuating. The more we have, the less satisfied we are. We seek to acquire more goods, but we fail to see that our spirit was not made to be satisfied by things. We forget that God provides for each of us according to our needs. It makes no sense to for-feit our peace and joy by spying through the fence at what our neighbor has, fuming with jealousy.

If we recognize in ourselves these character-deflating traits, these obstacles to concelebration, it is time to take stock of our understanding of the tenth commandment. We might be inclined to think it applies only to poor people, but it addresses deeper issues of consumerism, possessiveness, and acquisition at any price.

The disruptive scene when a relative dies and families gather around like vultures over carrion is one we either know from experience or can imagine: The aim is not so much to remember the dead as it is to snatch up goods and possessions that have been coveted for years. The memory of the one whose leftovers they are dividing, like the spoils of battle, is pushed into the background. The only thing that counts is the fact that "She promised me her fur coat!" And on and on the coveting goes. No one seems to think that someday others are going to fight over their corpse for the same coat!

The envy of the flesh, against which the ninth commandment warns us, is as debilitating as the jealous possessiveness, forbidden by the tenth.[1] Both forms of covetousness stem from our making things a substitute for seeking, finding, and fulfilling the will of our Maker for us.

An Eastern church father, St. John Chrysostom, who is oft quoted in *The Catechism,* says that instead of experiencing peace and joy, "we fight one another, and... unsettle the Body of Christ" [2538]. We see this tendency to covet, envy, and quarrel in children. "I want this. That's mine. You can't have it." Girls and boys fight in schoolyards and playgrounds over who gets to throw the ball. We still argue as grown-ups over silly things. The irony is that goods originally given to us by God can be the very cause of our separation from God. They create so much enmity between us it takes a lifetime, and then some, to overcome it.

CONDITIONS FOSTERING CONCELEBRATION

If the opposite of envy is admiration, then the opposite of jealousy is concelebration. This lasting character trait leaves no room for covetousness. St. John Chrysostom says it well: "Would you like to see God glorified by you? Then rejoice in your brother's progress and you will immediately give glory to God" [2540].

Aren't these the words we long to hear? Not "Who do

you think you are?" but "You're doing a good job. How happy I am for you!" The saint gives the reason why: "Because his servant could conquer envy by rejoicing in the merits of others, God will be praised" [2540].

To covet our neighbor's goods is to live in a perpetual state of comparison: Mary anxiously compares the dress she plans to wear to a wedding with the gown purchased by her friend. Is hers good enough? Will it make the proper fashion statement? John wonders if he will ever be able to play golf as well as the guy next door. How can he afford his kind of equipment? Where does he get the money to buy it? Comparisons like this exhaust the possibility of contentment with what we have. They compel us to acquire as much as we imagine others possess when they are probably behaving in the same way toward us.

People who lose themselves in jealous comparisons do not meet one another as persons but as collections of quantifiable goods. Competitiveness replaces compassion. They do not value people for their uniqueness and originality but for acquisitions that have nothing to do with who they are.

Commodities do not form good character traits. Good dispositions do. Instead of meeting people as people, we see only their possessions. And we are the poorer for it.

If we continue to compare ourselves with our neighbors, we can never be happy. We will always be trying to outdo them rather than growing in gratitude for what God has given us. Character formation comes to fruition when we keep our eyes on the inward, incomparable good that is ours by virtue of our substantial union with God. We value our original worth and avoid entrapment by joyless jealousy. We then look inward at our value in God's eyes, not outward at others' goods. The danger passes that we will spend our life mulling over disgruntled regrets. Now we see how much more there is to celebrate.

CAUSES OF COVETOUSNESS

Two aspects of originality can cause us to covet our neighbor's goods. One is invisible; the other visible. Unseen is the unique wellspring of original living, our being made in the form and likeness of God. Seen are the good things obtained by our original efforts—things like status, money, or success, possessions, positions, or promotion. Only gradually may it dawn upon the "person across the fence" that there is some connection between the neighbor's goods and the creativity and hard work that made such acquisition possible.

What the coveter really covets is the other's originality. Both who one is and what one has become objects of jealousy. What is absent in the coveter is often more upsetting than what others own. This missing good causes great pain in jealous persons. Soon their inner conflict spreads from eyeing enviously the success of certain persons to being jealous of all forms of unique self-motivation in society. Nobody should be different from nor have more than anyone else.

To the leveling mentality, inequality seems intolerable. The real source of one's inability to stop coveting and start concelebrating is repressed. Leveling is done in the name of equalizing everyone but in the meantime a society is crippled by lack of original contributions. Functionalism takes over with its stress on uniformity. The pursuit of excellence is eroded along with any expression of self-motivation. People not only covet others' goods; they covet the self they will never become.[2]

CALLED TO CONCELEBRATION

Covetousness isolates us from others. Concelebration marks a return to appreciation of uniqueness and a willingness to share our goods with one another. What the tenth commandment forbids is a dehumanizing force that erodes benevolence; what it offers as a counterforce to jealousy is a humanizing attitude of appreciative attention and gracious cooperation.

Concelebration hastens our redemption from isolation. It restores our appreciation of community while treasuring our unique gifts. Coveting depreciates the goods God created; concelebration appreciates the good wherever it is found.

This grateful vision generates peace and joy. It takes us to the heart and center of character formation—the divine initiative of love. God himself gave us the Ten Commandments to live by. Who are we not to follow his plan for our happiness? These directions are trustworthy. They make straight our crooked paths. They lead us to lasting consonance with God, self, and others. In their prohibitions and promises, we find a divinely crafted formula for spiritual wholeness no earthly wisdom can grant.

TIME TO REFLECT ON
THE TENTH COMMANDMENT

Step Ten: Concelebration

As the ninth commandment warns us against "envy of the flesh," so the tenth prohibits inordinate and jealous attachments to possessions that *must* be *mine*.

This commandment does not mince words when it comes to forbidding us to covet the goods of another. Without heeding the prohibition here proclaimed, there would be no deterrent to the theft, robbery, and fraud forbidden by the seventh commandment. The question is: Where is our treasure (see Matthew 6:21)? In our heart or in another person's pocket?

Jesus offers us an incomparable lesson in regard to the foolishness of avarice and greed. We would do well to meditate upon it, especially if we have a hard time celebrating the "enough" God gives to us every day:

> Therefore I tell you, do not worry about your life, what you will eat [or drink], or about your body, what you will wear. Is not life more than food and the body more than clothing? Look at the birds in the sky; they do not sow or reap, they gather nothing into barns, yet your heavenly Father feeds them. Are not you more important than they? Can any of you by worrying add a single moment to your life-span? Why are you anxious about clothes? Learn from the way the wild flowers grow. They do not work or spin. But I tell you that not even Solomon in all his splendor was clothed like one of them. If God so clothes the grass of the field, which grows today and is thrown into the oven tomorrow, will he not much more provide for

you, O you of little faith? So do not worry and say, "What are we to eat?" or "What are we to drink?" or "What are we to wear?" All these things the pagans seek. Your heavenly Father knows that you need them all. But seek first the kingdom [of God] and his righteousness, and all these things will be given you besides. Do not worry about tomorrow; tomorrow will take care of itself.

Matthew 6:25-34

This lesson reminds us that mere possession, no matter how much we have, cannot make us happy. As St. Augustine observes in *The Catechism:*

The Lord grieves over the rich, because they find their consolation in the abundance of goods. "Let the proud seek and love earthly kingdoms, but blessed are the poor in spirit for theirs is the Kingdom of heaven." Abandonment to the providence of the Father in heaven frees us from anxiety about tomorrow. Trust in God is a preparation for the blessedness of the poor. They shall see God [2547].

QUESTIONS FOR REFLECTION

1. Why are jealousy and covetousness apparently endemic to the human condition? How do I begin to eradicate these violations of the tenth commandment from my personal and social life? What am I doing to help young people to distinguish between "I want" and "I need"? How might in-depth spiritual formation, along with solid catechetical information, act as preventive medicine to the myth that amassing material goods will make us perfectly happy? What role does concelebration play in deterring covetousness?

Your Thoughts:

2. Will seeing a few moths eat away my stockpiles of material goods and a few worms bore holes in my "overcrowded-with-everything-money-can-buy" household be enough to teach me that lasting happiness is not found in things but in the God who made them? What must I do to make God the center of my life? When will his way have preeminence over everything I can buy or own?

Your Thoughts:

3. Do I believe that the most important condition for ascending to this tenth step to peace and joy is poverty of spirit? Am I ready, with the help of grace, to renounce all that I have for Jesus' sake and for that of the Gospel? (see Luke 14:33; Mark 8:35). Do I trust Jesus' promise that the poor of spirit are blessed by the gift of detachment— so blessed that the reign of God is theirs (see Matthew 5:3)?

Your Thoughts:

Your Concelebration Everywhere

You have granted each of us
A niche in human history
To blossom like a lovely tree
In the garden of humanity,
To listen ever more to life
As it unfolds and thrives
In space and time,
Not to whimper or whine
But to celebrate with humanity
Each victory over trivia,
Absorbing over millennia
The fiery lava of your grace
Flowing wave after wave,
From the volcano of God's flaming love.

We move in concelebration
With this earth ever changing
Like the skin of a mother
Slowly aging year after year
In the awesome panorama
Of exploding time and space.

To us you entrusted this tiny planet.
In your creation,
You set the timing
Of conception in the womb,
Of birth and of abiding,
Of listening to every happening
As a sweet tiding
Of your concelebration everywhere.

What makes us strong
Is not our self-same pride
But celebrating day and night
Any sign divine
Resounding in the field of life
You carved out for us so tenderly.

As grapes on the vine
We ripen on the tender stem
Of Bethlehem
Till we become a prism
Through which the glow of Christ's charism
Mellows humanity's malformation,
The stubborn fortification
Of hearts of stone,
Bitter and alone,
Filled with resentment
Till we flow in abandonment
Concelebrating his saving end
For our limping lives.

For all creation is a melody,
A song for God,
A song still open-ended,
An unfinished symphony.

—Fr. Adrian van Kaam

Epilogue

Only at the end of the Decalogue can we begin to appreciate the character-forming power of these ten divine commands. To obey or disobey one of them is to do the same for all. We cannot take one vertebra out of our spinal column and expect to stand up straight. Similarly, we need to live upright lives morally and to develop contemplative traits spiritually. Only then can we come to full maturity in soul, mind, spirit, and body. The commandments of God thus offer us the only true approach to wholistic or distinctively human formation. Through them, aided by divine grace, each of us can respond uniquely and communally to the universal call of holiness.

As we have shown in the preceding chapters and reflections, our faith and formation journey begins, in a sense, on our knees as we adore our God in himself. Only then can we venerate his name and dedicate ourselves to his Sabbath of rest and mercy. The character traits that sustain this growth in holiness are submission or humility; resurrection or the choice of life over death at all times; and confirmation lived in the context of chaste, committed love as single and married persons. Based on such advancements in our inner life, we can foster God-guided, Christ-centered, Spirit-inspired ordinary intimacy with people, events, and things through restitution, reconciliation, admiration, and concelebration.[1]

Thus in the Ten Commandments we have an ideal road map to spiritual and social formation, reformation, and transformation.

Martin Luther must have felt this way about the commandments when he wrote in *The Book of Concord*:

> Here, then, we have the Ten Commandments, a summary of divine teaching on what we are to do to make our whole life pleasing to God. They are the true fountain from which all good works must spring, the true channel through which all good works must flow. Apart from these Ten Commandments no deed, no conduct can be good or pleasing to God, no matter how great or precious it may be in the eyes of the world.[2]

In the end, what most facilitates these foundational steps to peace and joy is our desire to see God, which is to say, our desire for true happiness. How reassuring it is to know that to find this treasure we do not need to invent new steps; we need only to turn to the ancient, time-tested truths found in the Ten Commandments.

That is why the commandments, understood formatively, are not merely prohibitions. They are pathways to peace and joy that, according to St. Gregory in *The Catechism*, free us from "immoderate attachment to the goods of this world" so that we can find our "fulfillment in the vision and beatitude of God." "The promise [of seeing God] surpasses all beatitude.... In Scripture, to see is to possess.... Whoever sees God has obtained all the goods of which he can conceive" [2548].

God not only gives us the way to harmonious unfolding. He himself is the best reward we can attain for following the commandments with strength of character. That God may be our "all in all" is the reason we have written this book. Our hope, in the words of St. Augustine, is that "God himself will be the goal of our desires; we shall contemplate him without end, love him without surfeit, praise him without weariness. This gift [of a happy life and a healthy soul],... like eternal life itself, will assuredly be common to all" [2550].

Notes

Introduction

1. *Catechism of the Catholic Church* (Liguori, Mo.: Liguori, 1994): "The plan of this catechism is inspired by the great tradition of catechisms which build catechesis on four pillars: the baptismal profession of faith (the *Creed*), the sacraments of faith, the life of faith (the *Commandments*), and the prayer of the believer (the *Lord's Prayer*)" [13]. Hereafter abbreviated *The Catechism*, followed by paragraph numbers or cited directly in our text.
2. See paragraphs 2083-2550 of *The Catechism* for a detailed presentation of the Ten Commandments and their meaning for our Christian lives.

ONE
The Way of Adoration

1. Martin Luther, *The Book of Concord*, trans. Theodore G. Tappert (Philadelphia, Pa.: Fortress, 1959), 365-68. This edition of the Confession of the Evangelical Lutheran Church contains *The Large Catechism* in which we find Luther's thorough treatment of the *Ten Commandments*. All subsequent references to this work are taken from this edition, hereafter abbreviated *Concord*, followed by the appropriate page number(s).
2. In regard to the commandment not to have strange gods before God, *The Catechism* names a few of the "idols" that might command our attention if we are not careful. These are: superstition; divinizing or idolizing what is not God; divination and magic; irreligion; atheism and agnosticism [2111-2128].
3. To help you to answer this question, it would be wise to consult *The Catechism's* explanation of moral deviations and sins against the first commandment violating faith, hope, and love. These are: voluntary and/or involuntary doubt, incredulity and heresy, despair and presumption, indifference, ingratitude, lukewarmness, *acedia* or spiritual sloth, and hatred of God [2087-2094].

TWO
The Way of Veneration

1. For excellent insights into character and personality formation, see Adrian van Kaam, *Transcendent Formation*, Volume 6, Formative Spirituality Series (New York: Crossroad, 1995).

2. See John of the Cross, *The Dark Night* in the *Collected Works of St. John of the Cross*, Revised Edition, trans. Kieran Kavanaugh and Otilio Rodriguez (Washington, D.C.: ICS Publications, 1991).
3. John of the Cross, *The Spiritual Canticle*, Ibid., 535-537.
4. *Concord*, 372-374.

THREE
The Way of Dedication

1. This story is adapted from an episode narrated in a book entitled *The Power of Perception* (New York: Hawthorn, 1945), 135, by Marcus Bach. It is cited in John Killinger, *To My People With Love: The Ten Commandments for Today* (Nashville, Tenn.: Abingdon, 1988), 54-55. According to Bach, the "3Rs" of the Sabbath render it "a day of resting, a day of rejoicing, a day of remembering."
2. See Sr. Benedicta Ward, trans., *The Sayings of the Desert Fathers* (Kalamazoo, Mich.: Cistercian, 1975) for a closer look at St. Anthony's counsels for Christian character formation.
3. Here *The Catechism* also teaches: "The parish initiates the Christian people into the ordinary expression of the liturgical life: it gathers them together in this celebration; it teaches Christ's saving doctrine; it practices the charity of the Lord in good works and brotherly love" [2179].
4. See also Walter Ciszek, *He Leadeth Me* (Garden City, N.Y: Image Books, 1975) for a fuller treatment of what it means to live a life of dedicated presence to the Lord in whatever situation Holy Providence allows—from a prison cell to a suburban parish.
5. *Concord*, 376-377.

FOUR
The Way of Submission

1. For sage advice about formation for parenting, see Adrian van Kaam, *Transcendent Formation*, 81-93.
2. For a description of the "transcendence dynamic" and its place in human formation, see Adrian van Kaam, *Transcendence Therapy*, Volume 7, Formative Spirituality Series (New York: Crossroad, 1995). Fr. Adrian writes: "Our human spirit is marked by restlessness. It is our spirit that drives us relentlessly to go beyond, to advance, to transcend! The spirit's gift of openness to all that is keeps lifting us beyond what we already know, feel, try, do, accomplish, suffer, or enjoy. This dynamism of our spirit is a powerful source of ongoing character and personality formation, reformation, and transformation," 7.

3. Here is what the Holy Father says: "You parents, the divine precept seems to say, should act in such a way that your life will merit the honor (and the love) of your children! Do not let the divine command that you be honored fall into a moral vacuum! Ultimately then we are speaking of *mutual honor*. The commandment 'honor your father and mother' indirectly tells parents: Honor your sons and daughters. They deserve this because they are alive, because they are who they are, and this is true from the first moment of their conception. The Fourth Commandment then, by expressing the intimate bonds uniting the family, highlights the basis of its inner unity." See *Origins*, Volume 23: Number 37, March 3, 1994, for the full text of the Holy Father's letter.

4. Cited by David Hazard, *A Day in Your Presence: A 40-Day Journey in the Company of Francis of Assisi* (Minneapolis, Minn.: Bethany House, 1992), 107-108.

FIVE
The Way of Resurrection

1. See Killinger, 77-79.
2. Killinger, 79.
3. See *The Catechism* [2259-2317] for an in-depth analysis of what it means to respect human life and to safeguard peace.
4. *Concord*, 390.
5. As *The Catechism* states so beautifully: *"Human life is sacred* because from its beginning it involves the creative action of God and it remains forever in a special relationship with the Creator, who is its sole end. God alone is the Lord of life from its beginning until its end: no one can under any circumstance claim for himself the right directly to destroy an innocent human being" [2258]. For a discussion of respect for life in relation to health care, scientific research, and the dignity of the dying, refer specifically to *The Catechism* [2288-2301].

SIX
The Way of Confirmation

1. Killinger, 81.
2. Killinger, 90.
3. St. Augustine's struggle with lust, the war it stirred within his soul, is well documented in Books Eight to Ten of his *Confessions*.
4. See Pope John Paul II, *Familiaris Consortio* (On the Human Family), 11.

SEVEN
The Way of Restitution

1. For a thorough treatment of economic activity, social justice, and love for the poor in the context of the seventh commandment, see *The Catechism* [2426-2449].
2. *Concord*, 399.
3. *The Catechism* cites an excellent example of how it is that we recognize Christ's own presence in the poor: "When her mother reproached her for caring for the poor and the sick at home, St. Rose of Lima said to her: 'When we serve the poor and the sick, we serve Jesus. We must not fail to help our neighbors, because in them we serve Jesus'" [2449].

EIGHT
The Way of Reconciliation

1. Quoted by Thomas Merton in *Contemplative Prayer* (New York: Herder and Herder, 1969), 33. See also Susan Muto, *Pathways of Spiritual Living* (Petersham, Mass.: St. Bede's, 1988), 59.
2. For reasons why the social communications media must serve the common good rather than falsify the truth to exercise political control of opinion or in any way to manipulate the information in a free society, read *The Catechism* [2493-2499].
3. *The Catechism* adds to the call for reconciliation a reminder of the *"duty of reparation,"* indicating that "Every offense committed against justice and truth entails [this duty], even if its author has been forgiven. When it is impossible publicly to make reparation for a wrong, it must be made secretly. If someone who has suffered harm cannot be directly compensated, he must be given moral satisfaction in the name of charity. This duty of reparation also concerns offenses against another's reputation. This reparation, moral and sometimes material, must be evaluated in terms of the extent of the damage inflicted. It obliges in conscience" [2487].
4. *Concord*, 403.

NINE
The Way of Admiration

1. To understand this capital sin and its companion aberrations as treated by St. John in Book One of *The Dark Night*, see Susan Muto, *John of the Cross for Today: The Dark Night* (Notre Dame, Ind.: Ave Maria, 1994).

2. To better understand the relationship between "ascetism" (obeying the commandments) and "mysticism" (praying contemplatively), see *The Cloud of Unknowing,* edited by James Walsh, *Classics of Western Spirituality* (New York: Paulist, 1981).

3. Pope John Paul II, *Crossing the Threshold of Hope* (New York: Alfred Knopf, 1994), 223. Italics in text.

4. *Crossing the Threshold of Hope, 223.*

5. *Concord,* 407.

TEN
The Way of Concelebration

1. *The Catechism* explains the distinction between the tenth and the other commandments as follows:

   The tenth commandment unfolds and completes the ninth, which is concerned with concupiscence of the flesh. It forbids coveting the goods of another, as the root of theft, robbery, and fraud, which the seventh commandment forbids. "Lust of the eyes" leads to the violence and injustice forbidden by the fifth commandment. Avarice, like fornication, originates in the idolatry prohibited by the first three prescriptions of the Law. The tenth commandment concerns the intentions of the heart; with the ninth, it summarizes all the precepts of the Law [2534].

2. See Adrian van Kaam, *Living Creatively* (Denville, N.J.: Dimension, 1972). The original title of this was *Envy and Originality.*

Epilogue

1. See Susan Muto, *Late Have I Loved Thee: The Recovery of Intimacy* (New York: Crossroad, 1994).

2. *Concord,* 407.

Bibliography

Anonymous. *The Cloud of Unknowing.* James Walsh, ed. *Classics of Western Spirituality.* New York: Paulist, 1981.

Augustine. *The Confessions of St. Augustine.* John K. Ryan, trans. New York: Doubleday, 1960.

Bach, Marcus. *The Power of Perception.* New York: Hawthorn, 1945.

Catechism of the Catholic Church. English Translation. United States Catholic Conference. Liguori, Mo.: Liguori, 1994.

Catherine of Siena. *The Dialogue of Catherine of Siena.* Suzanne Noffke, trans. *Classics of Western Spirituality.* New York: Paulist, 1980.

Ciszek, Walter with Daniel Flaherty. *He Leadeth Me.* Garden City, N.Y.: Image, 1975.

Hazard, David. *A Day in Your Presence: A 40-Day Journey in the Company of Francis of Assisi.* Minneapolis, Minn: Bethany House, 1992.

John of the Cross. *The Dark Night* in *The Collected Works of St. John of the Cross.* Kieran Kavanaugh and Otilio Rodriguez, trans. Washington, D.C.: ICS Publications, 1991.

Killinger, John. *To My People With Love: The Ten Commandments for Today.* Nashville, Tenn.: Abingdon, 1988.

Lawrence of the Resurrection. *The Practice of the Presence of God.* Donald Attwater, trans. Springfield, Ill.: Templegate, 1974.

Luther, Martin. *The Book of Concord.* Theodore G. Tappert, trans. Philadelphia, Penn.: Fortress, 1959.

Merton, Thomas. *Contemplative Prayer.* New York: Herder and Herder, 1969.

Muggeridge, Malcolm. *Something Beautiful for God: Mother Teresa of Calcutta.* San Francisco: Harper, 1986.

Muto, Susan. *Blessings that Make Us Be: A Formative Approach to Living the Beatitudes.* Petersham, Mass.: St. Bede's, 1982.

___. *John of the Cross for Today: The Dark Night.* Notre Dame, Ind.: Ave Maria, 1994.

___. *Late Have I Loved Thee: The Recovery of Intimacy*. New York: Crossroad, 1995.

___. *Pathways of Spiritual Living*. Petersham, Mass.: St. Bede's, 1988.

___. *A Practical Guide to Spiritual Reading*. Petersham, Mass.: St. Bede's, 1994.

___ and Adrian van Kaam. *Commitment: Key to Christian Maturity*. Mahwah, N.J.: Paulist, 1989.

___ and Adrian van Kaam. *Divine Guidance: Seeking to Find and Follow the Will of God*. Ann Arbor, Mich.: Servant, 1994.

Pope John Paul II. "Letter to Families" in *Origins*, Volume 23: Number 37, March 3, 1994.

___. *Crossing the Threshold of Hope*. New York: Alfred Knopf, 1994.

Teresa of Avila. *The Way of Perfection* in the *Collected Works of St. Teresa of Avila*. Volume Two. Kieran Kavanaugh and Otilio Rodriguez, trans. Washington, D.C.: Institute of Carmelite Studies, 1980.

van Kaam, Adrian. *Living Creatively*. Denville, N.J.: Dimension, 1972.

___. *Looking for Jesus*. Denville, N.J.: Dimension, 1978.

___. *Roots of Christian Joy*. Denville, N.J.: Dimension, 1985.

___. *Transcendent Formation*. Volume 6. Formative Spirituality Series. New York: Crossroad, 1995.

___. *Transcendent Therapy*. Volume 7. Formative Spirituality Series. New York: Crossroad, 1995.

___. *The Woman at the Well*. Pittsburgh, Penn.: Epiphany, 1993.

___ and Susan Muto. *Practicing the Prayer of Presence*. Williston Park, N.Y.: Resurrection, 1993.

Ward, Sr. Benedicta, trans. *The Sayings of the Desert Fathers*. Kalamazoo, Mich.: Cistercian, 1975.